What readers are saying about The End of Software

Dr. Timothy Chou is one of the pioneers of the On Demand delivery model. His history and vision of the software industry's evolution should be required reading for everyone in software management. While promoting Oracle On Demand, this book's extensive sharing of experience actually benefits the whole IT industry.
David W. Yen, Executive Vice President, Scalable Systems,
Sun Microsystems, Inc.

Tim Chou redefines the way in which managers at all levels need to think about IT. In so doing, he defines the forces driving fundamental change in the software industry—creating both peril and opportunity for companies in the IT industry.
Michael J. Roberts, Senior Lecturer, Executive Director, Arthur Rock
Center for Entrepreneurship, Executive Director, Case Development
Rock Center 317, Harvard Business School

Tim has achieved his goal: a thought-provoking view of automation on automation-enabling services and an evolving world in IT delivery.
Jane Hollen, SVP, Xerox North America Information Management

On Demand software is changing the way corporations consume enterprise applications. In *The End of Software* Tim Chou presents a convincing case for this disruptive innovation by pinpointing the specific opportunities for increased efficiencies and improved reliability.
Greg Gianforte, CEO and Founder RightNow Technologies

There is a major change in the way enterprises use technology to enable their business processes in a highly efficient and cost-effective manner. Dr. Chou traces this shift from its early roots with big IT services outsourcers in the 1960s through to today's "software-as-a-service" delivery models that are fueling fast-growing companies such as Salesforce.com and WebEx.
Vinod Khosla, General Partner, Kleiner Perkins Caufield & Byers

The End of Software effectively answers the question, "What's next for the technology industry?" If you want to know where the market is heading, why it's heading that way, and how to best position your company for future growth, Tim's book is an invaluable guide.
Steve Printz, CIO, Pella Corporation

The End of Software is essential reading for anyone who wants to understand why the On Demand delivery model is what's next for the technology industry. Dr. Chou's deep experience with software as a service will help you discover how to best utilize this ground-breaking approach in your company.
Evan Goldberg, Chairman and CTO, NetSuite, Inc., One System. No Limits.

Dr. Chou's vision of the On Demand model is classic "division of labor" in the Adam Smith sense. Thermos embraced the On Demand model two years ago and have seen significant efficiencies in managing our IT systems, allowing us to better utilize our resources for supply chain improvement.
Alex Y. Huang, Ph.D., Chief Operating Officer, Thermos L.L.C.

For anyone looking to understand the market dynamics, *The End of Software* illustrates why the convergence of software, service, and the Internet will radically change the technology industry.
Jimmy Treybig, Venture Partner, N.E.A., Founder and former Chief Executive Officer, Tandem Computers

The End of Software is an invaluable guide for anyone looking to understand how they can operate software as a service at the speed and volume their business demands. As one of the pioneers of the Capacity On Demand delivery model, Dr. Chou clearly communicates how the convergence of software automation, grid computing, and the Internet is transforming the IT industry and delivering competitive business advantage.
Keith Morrow, CIO, 7-Eleven, Inc.

The End of Software articulates how the software-on-demand model holds out promise for reenergizing the technology industry by taming the life cycle of complex IT systems.
Gary Campbell, HP CTO Enterprise Servers and Storage

For anyone looking to make sense of the buzz around terms like *on demand, utility computing,* or *software as a service, The End of Software* paints a picture of why the convergence of software, services, and the Internet will drive new energy into the technology industry.
Rob Carter, Executive Vice President and CIO, FedEx Corporation

The End of Software is a wake-up call to management on the use of software systems. As software becomes a key engine of the economy, Dr. Chou explains how the On Demand delivery model will provide dramatic benefits to most organizations.
Dr. Jerry Held, CEO, The Held Group

The End of Software is a book with great insight and real experience behind it. As a pioneer in the world of software on demand, Dr. Timothy Chou offers his unique and valuable perspective on the next generation of computer software.
Min Zhu, President and CTO, WebEx Communications, Inc.

Many companies are looking for alternatives to the headaches of managing technology on a day-to-day basis, and *The End of Software* gives them an answer. Dr. Chou explains the inherent flaws of software, why it costs so much to maintain, and how your company can relieve the heavy burden. *The End of Software* is aspirin for nontech companies who find themselves at the mercy of technology run amok.
Nick Amin, President and Chief Operating Officer, CIGNA International Asia Pacific

The End of Software:
Finding Security, Flexibility,
and Profit in the
On Demand Future

Timothy Chou

A Division of Pearson Education
800 East 96th Street, Indianapolis, Indiana 46240

The End of Software: Finding Security, Flexibility, and Profit in the On Demand Future

International Standard Book Number: 0-672-32698-1

Library of Congress Catalog Card Number: 2004093271

Printed in the United States of America

First Printing: September 2004

07   06   05   04   4   3   2   1

Trademarks

All terms mentioned in this book that are known to be trademarks or service marks have been appropriately capitalized. Sams Publishing cannot attest to the accuracy of this information. Use of a term in this book should not be regarded as affecting the validity of any trademark or service mark.

Warning and Disclaimer

Every effort has been made to make this book as complete and as accurate as possible, but no warranty or fitness is implied. The information provided is on an "as is" basis. The author and the publisher shall have neither liability nor responsibility to any person or entity with respect to any loss or damages arising from the information contained in this book.

Bulk Sales

Sams Publishing offers excellent discounts on this book when ordered in quantity for bulk purchases or special sales. For more information, please contact

U.S. Corporate and Government Sales
1-800-382-3419
corpsales@pearsontechgroup.com

For sales outside of the United States, please contact

International Sales
1-317-428-3341
international@pearsontechgroup.com

Publisher
Paul Boger

Associate Publisher
Michael Stephens

Managing Editor
Charlotte Clapp

Project Editors
Tricia Liebig
Tonya Simpson

Production Editor
Megan Wade

Indexer
Chris Barrick

Publishing Coordinator
Cindy Teeters

Book Designer
Gary Adair

Page Layout
Brad Chinn

Preface

The End of Software might be an odd title for a book authored by someone who has spent his entire career in the software business. But in many ways we stand at the end of an era for the traditional software industry—the end to the traditional way we manage software, the end of traditional software development, and the end of the traditional software business model.

The traditional software model, in which we create the software, stamp it onto a CD, throw it across the fence, and wish the customer luck is dead. It will be replaced by sofware delivered on demand where networks collapse the distance between the producer and consumer of software. In many ways we are at the dawn of a change in the software industry no less significant than the change in the hardware industry that began when Intel introduced the 8080 microprocessor 30 years ago. The rate of change in the hardware industry was dictated by physics and manufacturing; this transformation in the software industry is limited only by our imagination.

Although Oracle isn't the only company pioneering this new model, as President of Oracle On Demand, it's the one I know best. Consequently, as you read further, you'll see many examples based

on successes we've had here at Oracle. We'll look at some of our experiences and innovations and how they've affected corporations
worldwide. We'll also examine what's happening in other traditional
technology companies, major research universities, and the latest
venture-backed startups. I hope you find the discussion to follow
both interesting and provocative.

Dr. Timothy Chou
President, Oracle On Demand
June 30, 2004

Contents at a Glance

Contents

Contents

About the Author

Dr. Timothy Chou serves as president of Oracle On Demand, the fastest-growing business inside Oracle. Oracle On Demand provides applications on demand for more than 250,000 corporate users globally. Users access ERP, CRM, HR, purchasing, supply chain, manufacturing, and business intelligence applications from more than 25 countries around the world on both public and private networks. Last year, Oracle On Demand processed over 175,000 expense reports; over 2,000,000 purchase orders; and over 5,000,000 sales orders. Under Dr. Chou's leadership, Oracle On Demand was recently recognized, along with IBM and EDS, by a multiclient Meta Group study as one of the top three companies customers are currently looking to today for application management and outsourcing services.

Not only does Dr. Chou lead a significant new business at Oracle, he is also recognized as an industry leader. He has been featured in *Forbes*, *Business Week*, and *The Economist*. In addition, he serves as a member of the board of directors of Embarcadero Technologies (EMBT) and as a member of the advisory board of WebEx (WEBX).

In addition to his tenure at Oracle, he was chief operating officer of Reasoning, Inc., and held numerous management positions at Tandem Computers.

Dr. Chou began his career after earning his M.S. and Ph.D. degrees in electrical engineering from the University of Illinois at Urbana-Champaign. He is the author of several publications in the area of scalable, reliable network computing and holds patents in this area as well. In addition, he has been a lecturer in computer science at Stanford University for more than 15 years and continues to give seminars.

Dedication

Dedicated to my parents Chou Yuan Pin and Suag Mei
En, without whose hard work and love none of this
would have been possible.

Acknowledgments

In the fall of 1999, I was having lunch with Gary Bloom, and he broached the idea of me returning to Oracle in some capacity. He mentioned that Larry Ellison was starting a new company called Business Online, which was Oracle's answer to the ASP boom. So, I met with Larry for two hours. Most of the time I argued about why he wanted to be in the business. "It's just a fat Exodus strategy," I kept saying. Although not fully convinced, I thought, "How many times does a large, established software company create a new venture? Maybe there is something to this idea of hosting Oracle applications."

Within six months it became obvious that this wasn't about hosting, or outsourcing, or managed services—it was about the future of the software business. Larry knew that then. Consequently, as I begin to acknowledge some of the key people who have made this book and this business possible, I begin with Larry. As you will see, in many ways he has fostered the software-on-demand model both inside and outside Oracle.

Starting any business is not easy. In fact, perhaps it is more difficult to start a business inside a large corporation than as a standalone. It takes a particular breed of people who can find what is good in a large corporation and blend it with the drive and focus required to make a fledgling business successful. From the earliest days, Gary Bloom, George Roberts, John Nugent, Donald Haig, Joseph King, Priscilla Morgan, Marian Szefler, Anil Thakur, Glenn Lim, Matt Yearling, and Ken Piro all contributed in many ways to getting the business off the ground. Our early customers were very supportive. They offered not only criticism—which they did freely—but also encouragement that we were doing the right thing. In early 2000, Carryl Smith, formerly of Triton Network Systems; David Chamberlain, formerly of Chipotle; David Lachicotte from CNLR; Kyle Lambert, vice president of Information Solutions at John I. Haas; Woody Muth at Kaverener Pulping; and Brenda Boyle at Empirix all took the time out of their busy schedules to help us be successful.

Our early successes met with some recognition. By late 2000, *Forbes* ran a story about this new model. I, of course, waxed on about this being the future of software, even predicting that "in five years every software firm must transform itself into an ASP—or die." Time has done little but strengthen that conviction. At the conclusion of the article, *Forbes* asked one of the most respected people in Oracle what he thought about my comments. "Tim may think that, but I'm not convinced," said CFO Jeffrey Henley. I knew my work was cut out for me.

Less than a year later in March 2001, Jeffrey Henley sponsored an event at the Palace Hotel in New York and invited the financial analysts community. From that day forward, Jeff has been one of the strongest advocates both inside and outside Oracle. His support has made all the difference. While we enjoyed success in selling mid-market customers in the United States on this new model, our objectives for 2002 were to move to much larger customers and to make the model work for our international customers. In Latin America, Luis Meisler and Alberto Chacin provided the leadership that enabled us to engage customers such as Posadas (the largest hotel chain in Latin America) and CVRD (the second-largest mining company in the world and largest market cap company in Brazil). Indeed, without the support of the senior sales executives—Derek Williams, Sergio Giacolleti, Kevin Fitzgerald, Keith Block, George Roberts, and John Nugent—the business would still be in startup mode.

Growing a business and reshaping a business model cannot be done without changes in pricing, business practices, sales compensation, and so on. Safra Catz and Jacqueline Woods provided the bridge between the traditional software models and this new world of Software on Demand. Without their support, much of this business would have remained forever on PowerPoint.

Although building software is not easy, managing software is an even greater challenge. When providing a service, you have to deliver every day, 24 hours a day, 365 days a year—there are no weekends or holidays. Mike Rocha, Mark Milani, Jean Reciyk, and Mark Iwanowski all have worked the front lines and back lines. In addition, while continuing to deliver a service, they have been aggressively reengineering that service and investing in the engineering required to move beyond people-powered outsourcing to computer-powered software on demand. Ron Wohl and Chuck Rozwat were also instrumental in bringing the right technologies, people, and processes to the table and making sure we continue to collapse the supply chain between the consumer and the producer of the software.

All this work, all this success, could have gone unnoticed without the efforts of marketing and communications. Lisa Arthur, Letty Ledbetter, Judith Sims, Mark Jarvis, Grace Chung, Carol Sato, and Paige O'Neill made the difference in getting the message out, which was no small feat given that the model we were pursuing was not what any of the other established software or service companies were doing. Key industry analyst Amy Mizoras Konary, IDC; Robin Bloor, Bloor Research; and Dr. Katy Ring, Ovum all provided viewpoints that have steadily helped the industry understand this fundamental change in the software business. They understood what we were trying to do, whereas many others were stuck trying to fit our vision into the traditional model. Thanks to Jeff Henley's active support of the new business, many financial analysts have also been supportive of our work and the fundamental business model. Jayson Maynard, Charles DiBonna, Rick Sherlund, and Bob Austrian all have seen the beginning of this fundamental shift. I like to think that Charles Phillips, who was an active proponent in his days at Morgan Stanley, joined Oracle because he liked the On Demand story so much.

No business can run without customers, and starting and growing a new business requires a particular kind of customer. Geoff Moore talks about the need to have "early adopters." Early adopters do not rely on well-established references in making their decisions, preferring instead to rely on their own intuition and vision; they are key to opening up any high-tech market segment. Software on Demand is no different. We owe a debt of gratitude to the early adopters: Richard Powell and Howard Aycock at Pepsi, Fred Magner at Unocal, Nick Amin at CIGNA International, Paul Brinkley at JDS Uniphase, Jame Dihonesto at Cabot Microelectronics, and Steve Pare and Karen Rubin at Bank of Montreal are just a few of those who had the courage and foresight to lead the way.

In the move from the traditonal software model to Software on Demand, much technology remains to be developed. The seeds of that lie in our universities. Ravi Iyer and Wen Mei Hwu from the University of Illinois, Armando Fox and George Candeda from Stanford University, Jacob Abraham from the University of Texas, and Roy Maxion from Carnegie-Mellon University have all opened their labs—and sometimes their lecture halls—to these new ideas. If we are to fulfill the ultimate vision of software as a service, it will be because the students of these and other universities invent the technology, products, and processes that will shape the new world.

Leading anything new can often be lonely. The difference between vision and delusion can be a fine line. It helps to be able to talk with others who share the same ideas. For that, I'd like to thank Jeff Bezos, Rick Dalzell, Min Zhu, Marc Benioff, John Cadedda, and Kevin Lo. Each, in his own way, has already blazed a trail. Each, in his own way, has led a change to the software business.

That leaves a small cadre of people to which an author (although I don't know as I deserve the title) is always indebted. Lisa Arthur and Glenn Lim took the time to read and comment on early drafts of the book. Michael Stephens, in a marathon session—he on the road, myself in Scotland—took a significant step in reshaping the book into what it is today.

And that brings me to one final person to acknowledge: my wife Sue. We met a long time ago when her racquetball partner couldn't make the date and she found me as a substitute. Throughout my career, she has been a firm foundation, first as wife and then as mom. Without her, I could never have found the time or the energy to take on these tough challenges that make life interesting.

Introduction

Twenty-five years ago, the high-tech business was small, computers were largely relegated to accounting, and the money major corporations spent on information technology barely made a dent in their overall budgets. Today that has all changed. High-tech businesses are some of the largest in the world. The Dow Jones Industrial Average includes four technology companies whose total market capitalization exceeds $600 billion. Computers have moved out of the role of accounting to managing supply chains, tracking manufacturing processes, and managing orders globally. There are even multibillion dollar companies founded and dependent only on information technology, such as Yahoo! and eBay.

With the increased role of computing has come increased spending to the point that global corporations' IT spending is no longer a rounding error. Today, we can estimate that the total spent on IT exceeds $1 trillion dollars per year. More amazingly, 75% of that is used for managing existing systems, most of which is dominated by the cost to manage the complex software that has been built over the past 25 years. Where does this cost come from? The increased usage of computing also brings increased exposure. Corporate costs for managing the security of computing is increasing each year. Today, most companies run 24/7; with no weekends or days off, managing the availability of these systems is a greater and greater challenge. And increasing dependence on computing also means an increasing need to change the environments. Some have estimated the cost to upgrade an enterprise application at $1,000 per user.

The disadvantage of this large expenditure on the operation of existing systems is that, with more than 75% of the budget being spent here, only 25% of the budget can be spent on new innovations. Unfortunately, the cost to manage past sins increases each year, so in time the amount of money spent on anything new will vanish—an alarming prognosis for any high-tech company.

Software as a service—or, as we will refer to it, *software on demand*—is the next step in the software industry. This isn't because it's a cool idea, but because it fundamentally alters the economics of software. If the cost of software (to a software company) can be reduced by a factor of 10, the shift in the software industry is as fundamental as the advent of the Intel microprocessor was to the hardware industry.

This book is full of examples and challenges to this transformation. Traditional software companies, including Oracle, are making the change, and new software companies such as WebEx are leading the way for next-generation startups. Read on if you think this will change your business. If you're the CIO or CEO of a large, medium-size, or small company and a consumer of software, you need to understand how this shift can change the economics of your IT budget and allow you to free up capital and resource to invest in the future, not the past.

If you're the CEO of a software company, you need to understand how the software on demand model changes your business starting in support, reaching into how you develop software, and culminating in changes to your fundamental business models based on a new economy. Finally, if you're an investor in high technology, I'm sure you wish you had bought Intel back in 1978. Key companies, both new and old, are participating in the move to software on demand. It's important that, as investors, you understand who gets it and who's pretending. The debate is not whether this shift in the software business will happen, only the rate.

1

Why Does IT Cost
So Much?

Dependence on IT is greater today than it has ever been. Think about it. Twenty-five years ago only the largest corporations relied on technology to support their growing global businesses. Today, every company—public or private, small or large, regional or international—uses IT in the front office, in the back office, and on the Internet. Even private individuals think nothing of using eBay and PayPal to sell goods to people half a world away, essentially making them small businesses outsourcing their IT needs to a sophisticated global vendor.

While our dependence on technology is growing, so is the cost. Estimates for the total spent on management of existing software reach *$1 trillion* per year. We've estimated the amount of money spent by 200,000+ Oracle customers to manage just their Oracle software at between $40 and $80 billion per year. Why does it cost so much to manage software? What is the cost of managing the change, performance, and availability of business systems? How much money should be spent managing software? And how can a CIO or CEO know that the money is being spent effectively?

Where Does It All Go?

The dramatic increase in IT dependency directly correlates to the increase in the money spent on corporate IT. Costs have skyrocketed to the point that CIOs charged with IT strategy and management are concerned. *CIO Magazine,* a U.S.-based publication for top IT professionals, reported in a December 2002 survey of CIOs that 67% of CIOs listed decreasing IT costs as their number-one business priority.

To understand the rising costs, you must understand how IT budgets are spent. In general, IT budgets today range from 1% to 10% of a corporation's overall revenue. However, more than 75% of the IT budget is spent just maintaining and running existing systems and software infrastructure. Gartner, Inc., published a report that summarized the typical IT budget as follows:

INFORMATION TECHNOLOGY INITIATIVE	% OF BUDGET
Support and maintenance of existing applications	36
Existing infrastructure	28
Administration	14
New development	21
Other	1

Source: Gartner, Inc.

The implication of the lopsided allocation of budget to maintaining the status quo of existing systems is grave. Take the following five companies and assume they spend only 1% of their total revenue on IT. Furthermore, assume that 79% of that budget is spent managing existing software. You get the following:

COMPANY	REVENUE (IN BILLIONS)	IT BUDGET	BUDGET FOR MANAGING EXISTING SOFTWARE
Cigna	$19.2	$192 million	$151 million
AMR	$17	$170 million	$134 million
Oracle	$10	$100 million	$79 million
Unocal	$6	$60 million	$47 million
Network Appliance	$0.9	$9 million	$7.46 million

These are huge numbers. Even with conservative estimates, just these five companies spend nearly half a billion dollars *per year* to manage their existing computing infrastructure. In the face of smaller or flat IT budgets and the need to continue cutting costs, precious few resources will be available for doing anything new, strategic, or innovative.

How Much Did I Really Pay?

Gartner, Inc., a global analyst firm tracking the high-tech market, points to maintenance and administration costs over time as a major culprit in the high spending required to maintain the status quo. "Customers can spend up to four times the cost of their software license per year to own and manage their applications," says Gartner, Inc.

Consider the implications of this statement. Assume you purchase software for a one-time price of $500,000. At 4 × the purchase price of the software, the cost to operate will be $2 million *per year*. Over 5 years, that's $10 million. So, the company is not making a $500,000 decision; it's really a $10.5 million decision. This cost multiplier is not limited to complex business software. Recently, "Microsoft said that the initial purchase is usually only 5% of the total cost of owning and maintaining a program."[1] Followed to its logical conclusion, this means that IT budgets might be stressed to the breaking point even if the initial purchase price of the software is $0.

Amy Mizoras Konary, a leading analyst on software licensing and delivery at IDC, cites five major areas that cost companies millions of dollars annually. "CIOs and their departments really focus on five key aspects to the management and maintenance of their computer and software systems: availability, performance, security, problems, and change management." Understanding the hidden costs behind these helps reveal the problems CIOs and their departments face.

High (Cost) Availability

Although the cost of availability management can be high, the cost of not managing availability can be higher. Let's look at a couple of recent high-profile examples. In June 1999, shares of eBay, Inc., plunged 30% in the wake of a site crash that cost the online auction house millions of dollars. The company revealed that the 24 hours during which its auction site was down was expected to reduce sales by 10% in the second quarter of that year.

Still not convinced? During the Thanksgiving holiday weekend of 2000, Amazon.com suffered a series of outages. Investment firm Thomas Weisel Partners estimated that one 20-minute outage deleted roughly 20,000 product orders and $500,000 in revenue. Although many companies might not be as dependent as eBay on IT, the cost of any outage can range from $100 to $10,000 per minute of downtime.

---

[1] *"Microsoft Wages Campaign Against Using Free Software,"* The Wall Street Journal, *December 9, 2002.*

Dealing with Disaster

Today it is not enough to spend money on protecting systems from hardware and software failures. After September 11, disaster recovery has moved up on the global agenda. Little data is available, but it is clear that regulated companies—finance, health care, pharmaceuticals, and government agencies—do a better job of protecting themselves than unregulated companies or even small companies. Those in a regulated environment might spend 1% of their IT budgets on disaster recovery. But is this enough?

Consider the implications of disasters on unregulated businesses. On September 11, Henry Schein (a $3 billion distributor of health care products based in Melville, New York) had no way to manage orders from the company's 400,000 customers around the world. Jim Harding, CIO of Henry Schein, changed the company's disaster services provider to IBM and added network capabilities from AT&T to back up systems, data, and other resources to IBM's offsite location, contracting with these companies to allow full recovery within 24 hours.

"We could have gone for a 4-hour recovery, which means pretty much every time you record a transaction, you're rewriting that to a disk drive at the IBM location," Harding explains. "We opted out of that because the cost is about 10 times what it is to do what we're doing. Now, if you're a financial institution, 24 hours might be the end of the world, but for us, it's okay." The company ended up choosing a less robust solution; nonetheless, it effectively doubled its security budget from 2000 levels.[2]

The Cost of Security

Protecting against physical disasters is not the only source of cost. The cost of ensuring a secure system has received increased visibility

---

[2]InfoWorld, *March 29, 2002.*

in the wake of the Melissa, Blaster, and Sobig.F viruses and worms. The cost to companies of these malicious viruses is estimated to be in the billions. *Investor's Business Daily* said worm and virus damage cost businesses up to $13 billion in 2003.[3] A recent example is Sobig.F, which in its first week blanketed the world with 200 million emails as it spread in attached files. While the cost of not paying attention to security is high, the cost of managing security is not trivial. A team at a Los Alamos laboratory estimated that, if they had to install a single security patch per month on their 11,000 desktop systems, it would require 27 people working full time, at an average of 19 updates per person per day.

Performance: Pay to Play

Security management clearly gets the front-page headlines, but there is also a significant cost to managing application performance. Consider the simple issue of managing disk performance. IDC estimates that corporations are losing as much as $50 billion per year as a result of not defragmenting every server and workstation on the network. Perhaps disk performance isn't being managed because the cost of doing so is so high. IDC estimates the annual cost per machine to run the manual disk defragmentation utility at about $2,000 (52 weeks × 1 hour per week × $40 per hour). For a network with 25 servers and 5,000 workstations, the annual cost would be $10 million, and that is assuming the company had the extra 250,000+ person-hours needed to do the job.

Change Management

Performance management is important, but it is not the sole source of IT spending. In change management, Gartner, Inc., estimates the cost of migrating from Windows 9x to Windows 2000 Professional at

---

[3] *Donna Howell, August 28, 2003.*

$2,015–$3,191 per desktop, dwarfing the $257 paid per seat license.[4] But the cost of change is not limited to the desktop. According to an AMR Research Report, "Minimizing ERP Upgrade Costs Require Synchronizing With Business Improvement Projects" (Bill Swanton, Dinelli Samaraweera, and Eric Klein, July 2004), "All upgrades involve steep fixed expenses, averaging over $1,839 per user and one man week of labor for every business user…The enormous labor resources necessary for upgrades are clear. On average, it will cost you one man week of project effort and $1,839 for each business user. This works out to 20.7 man years and $9.2M for a company with 5,000 business users…Small ERP implementations of fewer than 1,000 users averaged $4,155 per business user, almost four times the cost of large implementations."

So Where's the Good News?

The next chapter discusses the low-cost labor trap of traditional solutions. As it turns out, though, even if you could drastically reduce the financial impact of labor-intensive tasks, it wouldn't address the more crucial cost issues associated with maintaining availability and security or the lost revenues and opportunities associated with poor disaster recovery. Additionally, without the ability to innovate, companies risk watching more nimble competitors eat into their established markets.

Software on demand solutions address cost in several ways. First, by using well-established technologies as a platform for the solutions, the initial costs can be lower. Second, by automating routine tasks, maintenance over time can be less expensive without sacrificing availability, security, or fault tolerance. Finally, by basing solutions on a model that embraces change, upgrades become part of the normal flow rather than disruptive events.

---

[4] *www.serverworldmagazine.com, March 2003, softwarecost.shtml.*

Choosing Wisely

Strategic software systems are a valuable asset for the corporation and must be managed as such. But how do you know whether a system is managed well? How do you know if the IT budget is money effectively spent?

Achieving effectiveness across all five key areas of IT management can be a Herculean feat. Fortunately, some of the groundwork has already been established. One of the most important tasks in this process is finding a meaningful way to assess management effectiveness. The U.S. Department of Defense (DoD) had a similar challenge in the 1980s. The DoD was increasingly both purchasing software and having software built under contract, so it had to find a way to assess the quality of the software and ensure that the software was delivered on time and under budget.

The Capability Maturity Model

In 1984, the DoD competitively awarded the contract for the Software Engineering Institute (SEI) to Carnegie Mellon University in Pittsburgh. By 1987, the newly formed SEI published the first capability maturity model (CMM) for software. This was later expanded in Watt S. Humphrey's book *Managing the Software Process*. The fundamental underpinning of the CMM is that, if the software organization can gain control of the key development processes, high-quality software can be produced efficiently. Furthermore, these key software development processes can be characterized by the maturity of implementation. These fall into five maturity levels: initial, repeatable, defined, managed, and optimized:

- **Initial**—The software development process is characterized as ad hoc, and occasionally even chaotic. Few processes are defined, and success depends on individual effort and heroics.
- **Repeatable**—Basic software development management processes are established to track cost, schedule, and

functionality. The necessary process discipline is in place to repeat earlier successes on projects with similar applications.

- **Defined**—The software development process for both management and engineering activities is documented, standardized, and integrated into a standard software process for the organization. All projects use an approved, tailored version of the organization's standard software process for developing and maintaining software.

- **Managed**—Detailed measures of the software development process and product quality are collected. Both the software process and products are quantitatively understood and controlled.

- **Optimized**—Continuous development process improvement is enabled by quantitative feedback from the process and from piloting innovative ideas and technologies.

Predictability, effectiveness, and control of an organization's software processes improve as the organization moves up these five levels. While not rigorous, the empirical evidence to date supports this belief.

Measuring Operations

The CMM was designed to gauge and improve the development or creation process. The challenges change, however, once the software is in the field. As you will recall, the cost of deploying and maintaining the software is far greater than the initial purchase or development price. In this phase, the primary factors are the cost, quality, and effectiveness of managing or operating the software.

Leveraging the lessons from the SEI-CMM, Oracle has developed an operational model to focus on the key software operations processes: availability management, performance management, security management, problem management, and change management. Based on the experience of managing hundreds of software systems, a set of 10 key management processes has been identified. Oracle's rubric is far from the only one out there, but it serves to illustrate the issues you need to consider:

- **24/7 availability management process**—The purpose of 24/7 availability management is to ensure that a process is on hand on a 24-hour basis to manage the availability of the applications, database, systems, and hardware. Today, whether you have a small or large company, global business, purchasing, and manufacturing demands require that these systems be available 24 hours a day, 7 days a week, 365 days a year.

- **Disaster recovery management process**—Disaster recovery management ensures that a process from disaster to recovery is available in a predictable time. Applications and data should be synchronized. In these days of terrorist actions and with the advent of the Sarbanes-Oxley Act in the United States, this has become particularly important.

- **Security patch management process**—The purpose of this is to guarantee that, when a security patch is available from the software company, it is applied to the production systems in a known period of time. We all know the story of the SQL Slammer. Microsoft had the patch available for 6 months, but few operational systems had applied those patches.

- **Security audit management process**—Ensures that an external audit is performed at least once a year. Audits can be specialized or can adhere to standards such as the SAS70.

- **Capacity management process**—Ensures on a periodic basis that adequate hardware and software resources are available to deliver a specified level of application performance.

- **Resource management process**—The purpose of resource management is to ensure a process exists to add and shed infrastructure (people and computers) as load increases and decreases. Whether it's M&A, downsizing, or seasonal demands, no strategic system is static in its performance requirements.

- **Update management process**—Software update management ensures that software is updated at least once a year.

- **Production assessment process**—The purpose of this is to ensure that any change does not degrade the performance, availability, or security of the production systems.

- **Escalation management process**—Escalation management ensures a process exists from problem definition to resolution.

- **Proactive problem management process**—The purpose of this is to ensure a process is available to take high-priority fixes from the software company and apply them in a predictable amount of time.

Just as with the CMM, not only is the process important, but also the maturity of the process. It can be an ad hoc process, meaning if the system administrator or DBA comes in to work today, the process works, and if not, who knows? It can be defined, meaning you can read a document or process description language that describes the process. Conversely, it can be repeated, meaning the processes is repeated 10–100 times per year. It can also be automated; ultimately, any repetitive process can be automated, which is the key to higher quality and lower costs. Finally, the process can be optimized, meaning data from the process is used to change and improve the process. If you're managing a strategic software system, take the opportunity to evaluate how well a strategic application is managed by filling out your own report card:

KEY MANAGEMENT PROCESS	AD HOC	DEFINED	REPEATED	AUTOMATED	OPTIMIZED
24/7 availability					
Disaster recovery					
Security patch					
Audit management					
Capacity management					
Resource management					
Update management					
Production assessment					
Escalation management					
Proactive problem management					

Conclusion

Recently, the CIO of a mid-size U.S. company was talking about his IT budget, which is $20 million per year. Unfortunately, that was 100% allocated to managing the company's existing software systems. So, when a software sales representative shows up, he says, "I don't have any money." The odd thing is that he does—it's just all locked up. Without fully understanding the cost to manage IT and how to manage IT effectively, we could all end up in his shoes and it really will be the end of software.

2

What Has the Industry Done About IT?

Software companies have been busy for the past quarter century building software. Unfortunately, building that software has been a never-ending task—not unlike the great cathedrals of Europe. The downside has been that the complexity, incompleteness, unreliability, and constant change in software has driven enormous cost to the software consumer. Remember that 75% of all IT budgets—three quarters of a trillion dollars a year—goes to maintain systems.

The need to reduce overall costs within companies has driven executives to outsource IT management to external service providers. EDS is considered by many to be the granddaddy of the IT outsourcing business and is by far one of the largest companies of its type. EDS won its first outsourcing contract in 1963 to provide facilities management services for Frito-Lay. Success brought a listing on the NYSE in 1968, and five years later EDS reached $100 million in revenue. General Motors purchased the company in the mid-1980s. In 1994, EDS won a prestigious £1 billion IT outsourcing contract with U.K. company Inland Revenue. By 1996, EDS had split from General Motors and today is a $20 billion company with more than 125,000 employees.

EDS pioneered the IT outsourcing service model. In this model, the outsourcer takes over a client's hardware, buildings, and people and then focuses on running those operations more efficiently through basic cost control, vendor negotiation, and a focus on the bottom line. Typical contract lengths are long because the outsourcing vendor is taking on unknown risks in the existing operations and assumes it will be able to understand and operate more efficiently as time moves on. Historically, outsourcing services have been offered only to the very largest customers. Without a large enough contract and long enough time, the risks of the business model overshadow the benefits. As well, traditional outsourcing has been done entirely onsite with the primary skill set of successful outsourcers being project management.

The Race Is On

EDS's success prompted many competitors. In the early 1990s, IBM—at the time known primarily for mainframes and PCs—was struggling after years of lackluster earnings and strategic uncertainty. In 1993, the company's new CEO, Louis Gerstner, Jr., earmarked outsourcing and professional services as keys to IBM's financial turnaround. This division of the company, called IBM Global Services, had a distinct advantage over EDS. With IBM's portfolio of hardware and software products, IBM Global Services could build and operate single-source integrated solutions. By 1997, IBM Global Services had overtaken EDS as the IT services leader in terms of total revenue and organization size.

Today, IBM Global Services accounts for nearly half of the company's revenue and is IBM's most significant growth engine. IBM Global Services' revenue is now over $35 billion annually, up from

$4 billion in 1991 when the division was formed. The Global Service business is dwarfing even IBM's traditional hardware business and is nearly 10 times the size of its software business.

Although traditional outsourcers provide numerous advantages, they historically have met with several challenges. First is the question of how to provide flexibility. The basic business model leans toward fixing functionality to put an upper limit on cost. But businesses change. How can the outsourcing relationship change? Second, the traditional model is people-powered and therefore has a floor to the overall cost. Finally, even though you might be able to find lower labor costs at least temporarily, you must figure out how to provide reliable service when the fundamental vehicle for delivery is human labor. After all, humans are prone to human error. But there is hope, and it is buried in some fundamental principles: standardization, repetition, and ultimately automation.

Challenging the Status Quo

Many leading analyst firms have noted that numerous outsourcing deals have had problems because clients feel they are not being serviced properly and feel tied to a rigid, long-term contract. Outsourcing contracts need to be kept flexible and negotiated to allow for adjustments during the life of the contract.

At one time, the issue was what to outsource and which company to use as a service provider. But now the main issue is managing the relationship with the outsourcer. The Boston Consulting Group points to surveys indicating that managers often "reflect in hindsight that they seriously underestimated the complexity of structuring and negotiating a contract. Many respondents [to the BCG survey] feel they relied too much on 'establishing a good relationship' and got 'out-lawyered' in the process by the other party's legal team."

In other words, respondents to the outsourcing survey often feel that they have traded one management headache for another. The BCG report shows that if those involved in outsourcing are asked what they would have done differently, the answer given by everybody is to "have a stronger legal team." The next most common answer (90% of respondents) is to have a stronger contract management team. If the key issue is effective management of the availability, security, performance, problems, and changes in software, how can hiring better lawyers and contract managers achieve that?

Around the world, customers are asking the same of their outsourcers. Consultants contacted by *The Australian Financial Review* frequently mention the importance of the contract covering the outsourcing deal and ensuring it is kept sufficiently flexible. They say that the problem often arises when the original contract is negotiated as if the business were standing still. Changes in the size and composition of companies, changes to performance requirements, and changes to the underlying technology all present challenges to the rigid business models imposed by traditional outsourcers.

Traditional outsourcing agreements have involved the curious exercise of trying to think of all the things that could go wrong with a computer system, describing a mechanism to assess blame, and then calculating complex financial formulas to assess penalties. Lawyers are involved and, in time, these documents grow to hundreds of pages of legalese with dedicated teams to administer the contracts. A CIO of a Fortune 500 company commented, "Our contract is measured in feet, not words." In the days when a company handed over hundreds of people, real estate, and expensive computers, perhaps this was necessary, but it is most certainly an arcane way of doing business. No other service industry works this way. In general, you want to purchase the service, not get a penalty charge for the service not working.

The Human Factor

Traditional software management starts with the idea that it's all about people—the people at the service provider, such as EDS or IBM, or the people at your company. This focus has intensified as companies seek additional margin relief. However, you cannot escape the fact that people make mistakes.

People make mistakes. Even professional baseball players, highly trained over many years, make errors in 1%–2% of their fielding chances. Brought closer to home, data collected on the cause of failures in VAX systems reveals human operators were responsible for more than 50% of failures.[1] More recently, several researchers documented that human operator error is the largest single cause of service outages on the Internet.[2] Under stressful situations, such as installing an emergency bug fix, human error rates rise to between 10% and 100%.[3]

So, if this is the end of traditional software management, what's next? To move beyond people-powered software management, we must do four things. First, we must standardize the fundamental

1. B. Murphy and T. Gent. *Measuring System and Software Reliability Using an Automated Data Collection Process. Quality and Reliability Engineering International.*

2. D. Oppenheimer, A. Ganapathi, and D. A. Patterson. "Why Do Internet Services Fail, and What Can Be Done About It?" *Proceedings of the Fourth USENIX Symposium on Internet Technologies and Systems (USITS '03). Seattle, WA, March 2003.*

3. R.H. Pope. "Human Performance: What Improvement from Human Reliability Assessment." *Reliability Data Collection and Use in Risk and Availability Assessment. Proceedings of the Fifth Eurodata Conference. Springer-Verlag. April 1986.*

infrastructure and building blocks. After the building blocks are standardized, we must develop specialization and repetition of the key availability, security, performance, problem, and change management processes. Finally, if management process repetition exists, the process must acknowledge that computers are much better at repetition than people.

Repeat After Me...

The key to quality in any process is specialization and repetition. This is true for all human endeavors. Swimmers swim hundreds of laps to perfect a stroke and great surgeons perform hundreds of surgeries to master their craft. This is no different in the world of managing complex computer systems. Today, vendors like Oracle's On Demand business manage hundreds of systems and therefore have to repeat numerous processes multiple times.

Don Haig, VP Oracle On Demand, cites an example of where this repetition ultimately helps his customers, the users of Oracle applications. "Take software updates, an event that most organizations have to manage with some frequency and yet is an annoying distraction from their core business. CIOs really don't like to do updates but understand they need to stay current on the latest release of a vendor's software. When a customer is managing their own systems, they will do this upgrade once and only once. In Oracle On Demand, service upgrades have been repeated hundreds of times per year."

Upon hearing this example, Captain Kelley, CIO, Tricare Military Health Services, who was trained as a neurosurgeon, says, "You don't need to explain this further—we have an expression in my business: 'You don't want to be the first guy to get your cabbage worked on.'" However, in most IT departments today, complex tasks are done for the first time by people who read the book the night before.

A growing body of research is pinpointing the surgeons most likely to cause harm during surgery, creating benchmarks for obtaining safer medical care. A simple question posed to surgeons, the research shows, can often separate the talented from the average: *How often do you do this?* Research suggests that busy hospitals generally deliver better care. In fact, recent work cites the specific risks patients face in the hands of surgeons who don't frequently and regularly perform certain procedures.

"It is now a very legitimate question to ask a surgeon: How much experience with a procedure do you have? What are your complication rates?" says Tufts-New England Medical Center's surgeon-in-chief, Dr. William Mackey. "It's something every surgeon should keep track of and show patients if requested." Do we ask the same of our IT operations staff? How many times has the operations staff upgraded from release 1 to release 2?

Many studies of recovery from computer outages show that often the outage is extended because the operator has seen something out of the ordinary. Because it might be the first time she has seen the issue, she doesn't know how to react. Considering that most IT disaster recovery plans have never been tested, you can easily imagine how well disaster recovery will work when the time comes to implement it.

So, what constitutes a high degree of repetition? Dr. Mark S. Litwin, a University of California at Los Angeles urology professor, authored a study in which a high volume meant 40 or more procedures annually. Consider a corporation's system, network, database, and application operations teams—how many times a week have they performed a particular procedure? Is the procedure even written down? Can it be repeated?

Oracle's On Demand service has performed hundreds of upgrades from one release to the next. Today, these upgrades take 48 hours, plus or minus 2 hours. As with complex surgery, the repetition and specialization is leading to high success rates in the operation.

Automation

Ultimately, if a process is repeated, it can be automated. Automation of the key business processes in the business of managing software is the clear objective. Automating change, problem, security, performance, and availability management is key so that computers are driving the process, not humans.

But automate what? The idea is to automate the key IT management processes and the key availability, security, problem, performance, and change management processes. To better understand the idea of automating the key processes, we need only consider a simpler problem. If you went bowling 10 years ago, your first question (after "Where do I get a beer?") was probably, "Who is going to keep score?" or even, "Who knows how to score?" The same question was probably being asked in all 20 bowling lanes, each with a different answer to the question. So, even though all 20 lanes were bowling, how would a score of 200 on lane 1 compare to a 180 on lane 2?

Ten years later, the story is quite different. If you go into a high-tech bowling alley, you just type in your name and the computer keeps score. Now, you can be guaranteed that a score of 200 in lane 1 and a score of 180 in lane 2 would not be the same. This might not improve your bowling average, but you can be sure that the scoring process is implemented consistently. Consistency and standardization are all being enforced through automation.

A Brief History

Oracle began its commitment to the idea that software should be delivered as a service, not a CD-ROM, in 1999 with the creation of a separate company named Business Online. But Oracle CEO Larry Ellison, recognizing that the change was fundamental to Oracle's business—software—folded the company back into Oracle in 2000. While the name has changed from Oracle.com to Oracle Outsourcing and most recently to Oracle On Demand, the fundamental philosophy has been unwavering: Who better to manage Oracle software than Oracle? Today, the On Demand business is the fastest-growing business inside Oracle and has the goal of being a $1 billion business in less than 5 years.

Business Online began by providing customers an alternative to the management of the Oracle applications: the E-Business Suite, an integrated set of business applications including Finance, Human Resources, Customer Relationship Management, Manufacturing, and Supply Chain Management. Oracle also managed the complete stack surrounding its business applications, including the database, systems, and hardware. The implementation slice denotes the task of implementing the E-Business Suite for a given customer's business needs. Either partners or Oracle can perform implementations as long as they follow the engineered procedures defined in the Outsourcing Lifecycle. Partners, or outsourcing implementers, globally include KPMG, Cap Gemini, Atos-Origin, CSC, and Accenture.

Oracle's early customers were based in North America and were in general mid-size businesses. There were a large number of start-up companies, as well. The early going was full of challenges. Joseph King, Group Vice President of Oracle On Demand, was one of the charter members of the team. "Many customers were surprised to see Oracle get in this business. They didn't see how we could compete, and they were concerned that this was not a business Oracle would be committed to," said King, remembering the early days. In fact, Oracle remained committed to the business and began to evolve the fundamental model as it gained more experience with customers.

Location, Location, Location

The original model offered only the ability to locate hardware at an Oracle facility, but by mid-2000 the offering was extended to allow customers to choose the location and type of hardware. As the service continued to mature, there was a realization that for larger customers there needed to be the flexibility to extend and tailor the applications to the customer's business. In the early days of hosting its applications, Oracle had constrained the ability to change the software, offering a more vanilla approach to its E-Business Suite. Whether tailoring was adding a report or a form, or integrating the E-Business Suite with existing applications, all these represented software changes that needed to be added and supported in a Software on Demand environment.

Flexibility

To evolve this capability and deliver to its customers more choice in tailoring the software, Oracle defined a framework to categorize and codify changes to the software. The CEMLI (Configuration/ Customization, Extension, Modification, Localization, and Integration) Framework is a way to standardize and categorize virtually any change to the Oracle software. In fact, this framework translates into 19 classes of extensions that a customer might need to add to its Oracle system.

As adoption of its offerings grew, Oracle expanded its services to include offering its database and applications server as a service. This next level of outsourcing, called Technology on Demand, offers customers the flexibility to not only use CEMLIs to tailor the software, but also use independent software vendors (ISVs) and custom-written applications that run on the Oracle technology to provide more flexibility to solve their business needs. Several case studies are interesting. JDS Uniphase (JDSU) is the leading producer of optical networking components. At the height of the Internet bubble, the company was a multibillion-dollar corporation. But with the bursting of the bubble, JDSU was challenged to shave cost while maintaining the fundamental infrastructure required to allow for growth when the networking business turned around.

Long committed to outsourcing, JDSU chose to outsource the management of over 3,000 users of the E-Business Suite. This included 2,000 Manufacturing users; 1,000 Purchasing users; and over 500 CRM functionality users. In addition, several ISVs were required as part of the total solution. These software packages included PDM's manufacturing interface, Clear Orbit's warehouse management system, and Qiva's export compliance solution. In all cases, these applications run on the Oracle stack, with JDSU continuing to manage them and Oracle managing the technology underneath the applications. JDSU estimated that it has saved $35 million annually using the On Demand services from Oracle.

Unocal is an example of a forward-thinking company that is leveraging next-generation outsourcing to improve the speed at which its employees can get access to applications and information. Unocal was constrained by outdated software because it was running five-year-old versions of Oracle's business applications. To complicate the system, Unocal was also running a variety of additional applications, some of which were industry-specific and ISV-provided. Oracle provided Unocal with factory outsourcing services for its E-Business Suite and technology, helped bring Unocal to the latest release of its software, and is now working closely with Unocal to provide global access to information and applications for its 6,700 employees.

Although Oracle began its On Demand business in North America, in 2002 the company expanded its focus globally. In Latin America, Grupo Posadas (the largest hotel operator in Mexico and Latin

America with over 72 properties) became a customer. The company owns Fiesta Americana, Fiesta Inn, Caesar Park, Caesar Business, and The Explorean. The Posadas application footprint includes the Oracle E-Business Suite, ISV applications, and custom-written applications. The E-Business Suite supports more than 10,000 employees and manages in excess of 50,000 order lines.

Two ISV applications are a part of the solution: loyalty management from FMI and TLP's room/event reservation and pricing application. Both run on the Oracle technology stack. One of the most critical applications is the central reservation system written by Posadas. The applications are network-connected from Argentina, Brazil, Mexico, and the United States and operate in English, Portuguese, and Spanish. Leopoldo Toro, CIO at Posadas, commented, "While Posadas believes they have saved money by making this decision, more importantly the quality and level of service has been materially improved."

The On Demand Solution

Traditional IT outsourcing solutions have pioneered the idea that companies should focus on their core business competence and let service firms manage the IT systems. Although this is a good first step, there are many reasons the logical conclusion of this new direction is the end of traditional people-powered software management. The next generation of complex software management cannot be based on people; it must be based on processes and automation. The key availability, security, performance, problem, and change management processes must be identified, specialized, repeated, and ultimately automated. Only then can you be sure that change occurs with reliability, good performance, and security.

3

Location, Location, Location

The address of your corporate office might be the first thing that comes to mind when you think about your company's location, but should you also be similarly concerned about the location of your computers? Maybe one day in the future there won't be any discussion around the location of the computer. After all, who knows where the SABRE airline reservation computers are located? But until then there are real and perceived issues to be confronted. Many factors must be considered when making these decisions, including data privacy laws, networking predictability and performance, the political stability of the region, and the security and robustness of the facility. All these factors must be taken into account. In this chapter, we discuss the issues and some of the technical solutions being pioneered to allow users to choose the location of the computers, whether it's right next door or 6,000 miles away.

The Law

Let's start by considering international data privacy laws. Multinational firms that handle employee and customer data in Europe are finding it increasingly hard to quickly roll out new applications because of data privacy laws mandated by the European Union (EU). Across Europe, corporations must now pay a visit to the local data protection authority to disclose how marketing, human resources, financial, and healthcare data they collect is being warehoused, processed, or transported in or out of the EU. Moreover, these firms have to seek permission from worker-based organizations known as *works councils* to start new IT projects. Each of the 15 EU countries has adopted, or is in the process of adopting, slightly different provisions to satisfy the EU privacy directive issued in 1998 to promote harmonization of data privacy regulations.

European-based businesses acknowledge they must plan further in advance than they used to for IT projects. U.S. operations have to be sure they are abiding by European laws if they receive data on European subjects. The EU won't let data go to locations deemed to have inadequate data privacy laws, such as not giving European citizens the right to give consent for how data is shared or processed.

Some view the United States, with its freewheeling marketing practices, as generally inadequate in data privacy protection. At one point, it seemed possible that the EU might not allow citizen data to be transported to the United States. However, the EU and the United States reached a compromise with the so-called Safe Harbor agreement.

Any Port in a Storm

Safe Harbor was established in 2000, and it is designed to provide legal protection to U.S. companies and organizations that, as part of their European operations, gather personal data about people living there, including employees and customers. Companies that sign up for Safe Harbor avoid the prospect that the EU might perfunctorily shut down their network operations from Europe. With Safe Harbor, the EU can spot-check and, if it doesn't like what it sees, it can complain to the Federal Trade Commission. Over 100 firms have signed up for Safe Harbor.

It's not perfect, however. Woe to those who run afoul of the data police, which can mete out fines and even cut off data flow if they wish. When Microsoft quarreled with Spanish authorities over user data it had collected for its Windows 98 rollout, Spain slapped Microsoft with a monetary fine. Microsoft, like a growing number of other firms, has joined Safe Harbor to assure Europe of its adequacy in data protection and, more importantly, to keep business running smoothly.

The intent of the European Commission (EC) Data Protection Directive has moved to other countries. In particular, countries with data privacy legislation include Australia, Hong Kong, and New Zealand. In Mexico, the Federal Law to Protect Personal Data was approved by the Mexican Senate on April 30, 2002. The senate-approved version of Mexico's data privacy law is modeled on Spain's data protection law.

As electronic commerce grows, new laws, regulations, and standards are being established that force the IT department to be not only technology experts, but also legal and security experts. As with software installations, working with an expert who understands the present and future issues can save a lot of expensive trial and error.

Connecting the Wires

Legal concerns aren't the only issues that influence your choice on where to locate your computers. If network bandwidth were free, ubiquitous, reliable, and secure, the location of computers would technically not matter. However, bandwidth isn't free. While the industry has made great strides, we still have a long way to go. We have the public Internet, which is ubiquitous and cheap, but it's far from a corporate-quality network.

It's one thing to rely on the Internet for Web sites and email. As a corporate network infrastructure, however, both its security and reliability can sorely disappoint. Network security breaches are escalating in both number and complexity. CERT says that more than 76,000 security incidents were reported in the first half of 2003 and are on track to grow 600% from 2000 levels.

Denial-of-service (DoS) attacks are of particular concern because, even without compromising your security, a malicious individual can bring an Internet location to its knees. This can be particularly painful if it is a key component of your corporate network.

This type of attack is effective because the Internet is composed of limited and consumable resources and Internet security is highly interdependent. DoS attacks use multiple systems to attack one or more victim systems with the intent of denying service to legitimate users. The degree of automation in attack tools enables a single attacker to install his tools and control tens of thousands of compromised systems for use in attacks. Intruders often search address blocks known to contain high concentrations of vulnerable systems with high-speed connections. Intruders planning to install their attack tools increasingly target cable modem, DSL, and university address blocks.

Various other threats lurk on public network channels. Worms, viruses, and other malicious code can weasel their way into your system if it's not adequately protected. Inexpertly configured systems that your data might encounter on its way to its final destination pose another threat. You can suffer collateral damage due to a failure or an attack whose epicenter is hundreds or thousands of miles away.

Infranet: A Corporate-Quality Internet

Historically, implementing private corporate networks has addressed many of the challenges of security, performance, and change management. However, private corporate networks are not ubiquitous and far from cheap. Pradeep Sindhu (founder and co-chairman of Juniper Networks) says, "Unfortunately, today's corporate networks are engineered for one network, one application. That uniqueness drives up cost and slows the ability for customers to take advantage of the benefits of global networking."

Sindhu is driving a networking industry initiative to address this issue. The fundamental thesis is that conventional private or public networking approaches cannot solve today's challenges. The solution is neither a public Internet nor a private network infrastructure; it is the best of both. The solution Sindhu proposes is an infranet. An *infranet* is a move away from closed private networks and proprietary solutions to selectively open networks and industry collaboration. It is composed of three fundamental building blocks. The first, called user request, is an expected experience driven by the user's application. It enables users to automatically get the experience they require based on the application they are using. In the infranet, the application dynamically requests the level of security, quality, and bandwidth it requires from the network.

The second building block is predictability throughout the network: Assured delivery provides a network foundation to ensure that services are delivered throughout the network with the specifications required by the user request. This predictable experience is critical for enabling any real-time communications, including Web conferencing, camera phones, collaboration, and other applications.

Finally, an infranet requires a realistic implementation for next-generation mass-market communication: Carrier connections are required to make global services economically viable. Just as the industry has developed successful carrier connections for voice and mobile networks, the same must be done on the public network so new services are not gated by each carrier's global expansion.

Back to Why Location Matters

All that being said, in the absence of a low-cost, universally available, well-managed network, location continues to matter. Or, put more simply, there are times when you can't be too close to your servers. For example, certain applications demand much higher bandwidth and lower latency than others. Call center applications, for instance, require that the computers be located near the telephone switches.

Also consider that not all companies are global. Some regional companies, such as Producto Fernandez, the second-largest sausage manufacturer in Chile, conduct 100% of their transactions within their country. It makes no sense for Producto Fernandez to run an expensive network up to the United States and back down to Chile. It makes more sense to move the computers to the edge of the network.

For a global company, however, computers arguably are best located in the middle of the United States. It's seismically safe, has high-quality power, has low-cost real estate, is politically stable, and has large networking capacity. Although a good street address is important, you also must consider the quality of the real estate, or the quality of the physical infrastructure.

What Are You Made Of?

It is important to remember that a typical data center site is composed of many mechanical, electrical, fire protection, security, and other systems, each of which has additional subsystems and components. For a business-critical application, the facility should at least have an ability to control physical access. For example, in Oracle's primary data center located in Texas, the outer walls can withstand a semi-truck hitting the wall at 60 mph. While one hopes this never happens, it does provide a meaningful measure of protection against unwanted physical access to the building. In addition, embassy-grade baleens are raised and lowered to control vehicle entry. Full-time camera and armed guard surveillance monitors the approaches to the building, with physical access controlled by a combination of biometric devices and mantraps.

Physical security management is critical, but it's equally important for availability management to have high-quality power. At a minimum, the facility should be capable of operating for a fixed period of time when power is lost to allow for graceful shutdown. For mission-critical applications, the demands go further. A power outage in Memphis shouldn't affect users in Dallas or Los Angeles, much less in London, Tokyo, or Sydney.

A world-class data center has sufficient backup batteries and diesel fuel generators onsite to run uninterrupted for 72 hours. The facility would include measures to modify the site infrastructure activity without disrupting the computer hardware operation in any way. Such upgrades would include preventive and programmable maintenance, the repair and replacement of components, the addition or removal of capacity components, the testing of components and systems, and more.

As an example, for large sites using chilled water for cooling, this means two independent sets of pipes. Sufficient capacity and distribution must be available to simultaneously carry the load on one path while performing maintenance or testing on the other path. The physical infrastructure is important and forms the basis for high-quality management; many such facilities exist around the world today. A reliable and secure physical and networking infrastructure is a fundamental requirement for modern computing.

My Place or Yours?

Technical, business, and social demands all factor together in driving the choice of location. Depending on individual situation and the availability of adequate facilities in your region, you will need to make the critical decision of where to locate the computers to accomodate a flexible solution. Oracle's On Demand manages Oracle software either in a location Oracle chooses (@Oracle) or in a location the customer chooses (@Customer). We'll look at the parameters of each of these models as an illustration of why you might select one over the other. We'll also address the way Software on Demand design principles factor into each choice.

My Place

In the @Oracle model Oracle has chosen to locate the servers in the middle of Texas. A secure network link between Oracle's data center and the customer's site supports the transmission of application transaction traffic from the end user to the computers. The aforementioned data center has all of the qualifications of a world-class data center.

Beyond the location, in the @Oracle model, Oracle also selects the computers. The computer configuration on which Oracle On Demand has standardized is a Linux Intel grid architecture with network attached storage. The On Demand grid computer allows the use of many low-cost, high-performance servers to form one large computer that can be shared on demand. Let's take a look at one example of a customer using the @Oracle model.

Commercial Net Lease Realty @Oracle

Commercial Net Lease Realty (CNLR) is a real estate investment trust traded on the New York Stock Exchange. The company acquires, sells, and manages single-tenant commercial buildings leased by such retail chains as Target, Barnes & Noble, and Bennigan's. At any one time, its portfolio might hold 350 properties in 38 states.

Although the company's management was financially sophisticated, the systems it relied on were not. By 1999, it was clear that CNLR had to overhaul its management information system to redesign business processes so it could generate savings and increase productivity. CNLR solicited proposals from four software vendors, three of which worked solely in financial services. The company ultimately opted for an Oracle installation using the Oracle Assets, Oracle Cash Management, Oracle Financial Analyzer, Oracle Internet Expenses, Oracle General Ledger, Oracle Payables, Oracle Receivables, Oracle Purchasing, Oracle Projects, and Oracle Property Manager applications.

With its business based in North America, choosing the @Oracle model was not difficult. David Lachicotte, CIO at CNLR, saw the benefits of standardization and made a bet that the Oracle On Demand model could return a significant reduction in IT cost while increasing functionality.

CNLR realized more than $2.04 million in savings over the first three years of its operation. This represented an 84% annual reduction in hardware, software, professional services, and continuing cost spending from the company's information technology budget, for a return on investment of 136%. More important, it has a system that separates core from context. The solution reflects the sophistication of its underlying business, allowing CNLR to focus on real estate operations and not computing infrastructure.

Your Place

While the vendor-hosted model works for many companies, some technical and legal scenarios demand greater flexibility. With modern networking technology, the location of the computer should be irrelevant. At some point of the day or night, on a 24/7 basis the people managing the computer will be remote from the physical location of the computer. In the Software on Demand model, it's a relatively simple matter to then give the customer the option of choosing the location and type of system. The key to the customer-hosted model, however, is once again standardized hardware and software. In the Oracle @Customer model, that includes modern hardware supporting HP-UX from HP, Solaris from Sun, and AIX from IBM. If the customer chooses equipment that conforms to these standards, it can realize benefits in security, flexibility, and availability similar to those offered by a vendor-hosted solution. In either case— independent of location of the computers—the availability, performance, security problems, change, and availability are managed 24/7. How can this be? The basic service model is designed to be 24/7. This is implemented by locating the people managing the system in the Americas, Asia, and Europe. Given this basic design, it can't matter where the computers are located.

Charles Marcus @Customer

For the sake of comparison, here's an example of an E-Business Suite On Demand @Customer solution. Established in London in 1977 as a chartered accounting organization, Charles Marcus extended its operations in 1984 to include management consulting in Europe. The Sydney office opened in 1996. Unlike most professional services firms, Charles Marcus employs consultants who work as independently as possible. Although the consultants select and manage their own projects, mainly the design and implementation of enterprise applications, Charles Marcus bills the client and pays the consultant a salary subject to local payroll taxes.

With plans to expand operations in Europe and Southeast Asia, Charles Marcus realized it needed to upgrade its business systems to support multiple currencies and online access to applications. Its legacy system had no support for multiple currencies. Billing in currencies other than the pound sterling (GBP) was prepared manually and entered in GBP at spot rates of conversion. Expanding in new markets would have demanded time-consuming manual conversions, putting a strain on the company's billing staff. They knew that the increased volume and complexity of expanded operations would push its fragmented legacy systems to the breaking point, so a single, consolidated system was a must. All of this led to the choice to move to Oracle's applications—the E-Business suite.

With so much of the Charles Marcus application usage centered in Australia, it made sense to locate the computers in Australia. Using the @Customer model, Charles Marcus selected Hostworks of Adelaide Australia to purchase and house the servers in Australia. Given the power of the Oracle On Demand model, these standardized servers could be managed reliably by Oracle engineers thousands of miles away.

Conclusion

In a world where trade is increasingly electronic, many international customers prefer to have control of the physical infrastructure. Software on Demand services must provide the flexibility to locate hardware anywhere in the world and allow the customer to balance the complex legal and technical issues in making the right decision.

Now that you know how to locate the computers, let's move on to the challenges of managing them. The next five chapters are devoted to individually discussing the challenges of managing security, availability, performance, problems, and change in complex software environments. Within each chapter, various computer-powered software solutions are discussed. Some of these are being implemented today in production systems; some are still in the research phase at some of the world's best universities. All are part of the fabric of the steps we must take.

4

It's About the Performance

When mission-critical applications are overloaded with data, are swamped by user requests, or experience any of a number of other situations or events that negatively affect them, their slow performance can severely impact a company's bottom line. That much you know already. Time spent waiting for the computer to cough out an answer is, essentially, wasted. The challenge of designing, building, sizing, deploying, and managing high-performance, cost-effective solutions has long been pursued in the industry.

Many traditional means have depended on having smart people with slide rules to make estimates and forecast on both how to characterize the workload generated by a user and how to estimate the capabilities of a particular software and hardware configuration. We'll discuss some of these methods in brief, but clearly in the face of increasingly complex systems, there must be a better way. Moving from people-powered to computer-powered performance management is at the root of many modern innovations in what is being widely discussed as *grid computing*. We'll show you some of the innovative work being done at EMC, Sun, HP, Google, and Oracle to take advantage of increasing standardization and automation to reduce costs and increase the performance management service levels.

The fundamental material in this chapter gets a little geeky if you're a corporate executive or employee who utilizes your systems and view that access as a service. But if you're developing the Software on Demand products, you need to understand what has become possible.

Cost of Poor Performance

Let's start with a basic call center customer service scenario. Suppose your call center has 2,000 agents taking 25–50 calls per agent, with a total of 50,000–100,000 calls per day. Due to volume, your database overloads and slows response times for queries, inserts, and updates by 5 seconds per operation. If a typical customer inquiry requires five database operations, the slow system performance causes a total of 25 seconds of idle time with each call.

This 25-second delay amasses 300–700 agent hours of lost productivity every day. Unless you improve the performance of your system, the only way to improve customer hold time or manage larger call volumes is to hire more agents—resulting in higher operating costs and lower margins. At this point, a call center based in China or India starts to look pretty good.

Throw Another Box at It

Given the relatively inexpensive initial cost of acquisition, the focus on performance often results in companies overstocking their hardware infrastructure. I recently heard about a consultant hired by a U.S. company to study its IT infrastructure. The company had three locations with a total of 900 servers. The consultant started looking at the workloads and the utilization of each server and discovered that there was only *one* business application per server. According to the system administrators, the company had tried to run more than one application, but the results were poor perform-ance. The application administration people started pointing fingers at each other, each claiming the problem was with the other applica-tion. The result? One application, one server.

Tremendous cost is buried in underutilized server infrastructure. This waste is equally apparent when you look at disk utilization. Many studies today indicate that average disk utilization is below 50%, meaning half of the storage infrastructure is unnecessary.

How Much Do You Need?

Traditional solutions to performance management start with system sizing. The classic approach is to use analytic modeling or simula-tions to determine whether you have enough hardware. Typically the user is asked, "How many transactions do you expect to do this year and how many next year?" Using Excel and a little black magic, the performance expert kicks out an answer like "eight CPUs and 700GB of disk." Analytic models rely on everything from simple Excel spreadsheets to exotic queuing models, but virtually all suffer from the inability to accurately characterize both the arrival patterns of work and the service times for a particular transaction.

Simulation is the other traditional approach. In this approach, a synthetic workload is generated and run on benchmark hardware. This is very costly; however, for large procurements the hardware vendors and the customers often invest the time and effort. Of course, they are faced with a similar problem: Can they accurately characterize the workload and simulate the arrival patterns? As with all models, garbage in = garbage out.

I Want It Now

In the early 1980s, the industry began a race that has accelerated over time: the automation of daily end-user business transactions. The first application that received widespread focus was the automated teller transactions that form the backbone of the instant-money machines found in virtually every bank, airport, and convenience store. In recent years, we've seen this automation trend ripple through almost every area of business, from grocery stores to gas stations. As opposed to the batch-computing model that dominated the industry in the 1960s and 1970s, this new online model of computing had relatively unsophisticated clerks and consumers directly conducting simple update transactions against an online database system. Thus, the online transaction processing (OLTP) industry was born, and it's an industry that now represents billions of dollars in annual sales.

Given the stakes, the competition among OLTP vendors is intense. But, how do you prove who is the best? The answer, of course, is a test, or a *benchmark*. Beginning in the mid-1980s, computer system and database vendors began to make performance claims based on the TP1 benchmark, a benchmark originally developed within IBM that then found its way into the public domain. This benchmark purported to measure the performance of a system handling ATM transactions in a batch mode without the network or user interaction (think-time) components of the system workload.

The TP1 benchmark had two major flaws, however. First, by ignoring the network and user interaction components of an OLTP workload, the system being tested could generate inflated performance numbers. Second, the benchmark was poorly defined and there was no supervision or control of the benchmark process. As a result, the TP1 marketing claims, not surprisingly, had little credibility.

Enter DebitCredit

In the April 1985 issue of *Datamation*, Jim Gray—in collaboration with 24 others from academy and industry—published (anonymously) an article titled, "A Measure of Transaction Processing Power." This article outlined a test for online transaction processing, which was given the title of DebitCredit. Unlike the TP1 benchmark, Gray's DebitCredit benchmark specified a true system-level benchmark in which the network and user interaction components of the workload were included. In addition, it outlined several other key features of the benchmarking process.

First, the total system cost must be published with the performance rating. Total system cost includes all hardware and software used to successfully run the benchmark, including 5 years' maintenance costs. Until this concept became law in the TPC process, vendors often quoted only part of the overall system cost that generated a given performance rating.

Second, the test must be specified in terms of high-level functional requirements rather than specifying any given hardware or software platform or code-level requirements. This allowed any company to run this benchmark if it could meet the functional requirements of the benchmark.

Third, the benchmark workload must scale up, meaning the number of users and size of the database tables must be increased proportionally with the increasing power of the system to produce higher transaction rates. The scaling prevents the workload from being overwhelmed by the rapidly increasing power of OLTP systems. Finally, the overall transaction rate must be constrained by a response time requirement. In DebitCredit, 95% of all transactions must be completed in less than 1 second.

While this effort met with some success, in the end many pointed out that the simple DebitCredit benchmark did not represent all real-world workloads. What followed were TPC-A, TPC-B, TPC-C, TPC-D, and TPC-W, each of which attempted to characterize a different type of workload. As with all games, more rules were put in place to ensure everyone was playing fairly.

The effort still continues, but it appears to have run its course and customers are still left with the challenge of how to manage performance and how to size systems and resources appropriately. Or, put another way, it's hard to know what to expect out of your new system when you don't know exactly how to measure the performance of your old one.

Waste Not, Want Not

Rapid improvements in communications and computing technologies are leading many to consider more innovative approaches to getting effective computing power. Many in the scientific community have observed that there are more than 400 million PCs around the world, many as powerful as an early 1990s supercomputer, and most are idle most of the time. In 1985, Miron Livny showed that most workstations are often idle and proposed a system to harness those idle cycles for useful work. This basic idea is the foundation of what we now call *grid computing*.

In 1997, Scott Kurowski established the Entropia network to apply idle computers worldwide to scientific problems. In just 2 years, this network grew to encompass 30,000 computers. Among its several scientific achievements is the identification of the largest known prime number.

The next big breakthrough in grid computing was David Anderson's SETI@home project. This enlisted personal computers to work on the problem of analyzing data from the Arecibo radio telescope for signatures that might indicate extraterrestrial intelligence. SETI@home is now running on half a million PCs. In this case individual users allow SETI to use their personal computer to run an analysis whenever the PC is idle. This is done by linking the work unit to a SETI screensaver. New philanthropic computing activities have started including Parabon's Compute Against Cancer, which analyzes patient responses to chemotherapy, and Entropia's FightAidsAtHome project to evaluate prospective targets for drug discovery.

The one advantage the scientific computing community has is that a typical problem is computationally bound and can be simply partitioned, whereas in business, problems are usually database bound and cannot be simply partitioned. Nevertheless, the concepts on which scientific grid computing was founded are being applied to the world of enterprise computing.

An Appropriate Response

Just as in scientific computing, most enterprise computers are woefully underutilized. This has often been the case because of the belief that the user must prioritize and configure a system for her individual needs. Not wanting to risk being undersized, the typical reaction was to buy more than you needed.

In traditional IT outsourcing, any changes to the environment are accompanied by a change request, reviewed by a change management committee, and typically result in an additional service fee. Computer-powered performance management takes a completely different view. Rather than trying to use Excel to predict the future, the Software on Demand model approach demands that systems be designed to accept change gracefully. That way, you simply respond to changes in demand and allocate more resources as necessary.

The idea of providing new mechanisms for managing hardware infrastructure for higher performance shows up in many ways. VMWare, recently acquired by EMC, has designed technology to provide single server virtualization. Additionally, Sun, HP, and IBM have all launched grid computing initiatives to manage multiple computers. Let's take a look at how this might work in practice.

The Server Is Where?

"The development servers stached under programmers' desks were the last straw," says Bob Armstrong. He's the IT director at Delaware North, a diversified hospitality, food service, and retail company that's also one of the largest privately held businesses in the United States. In early 2002, Delaware North's Buffalo headquarters faced a common problem. Its roster of Windows NT servers had mushroomed to 36; the data center had been designed for 15.

"The software vendors all wanted their applications on a separate server," Armstrong says. "We ran out of space." Hence, the development servers were shoved under desks "...and we were exceeding our air conditioning limits." Armstrong and Delaware North's CIO pegged the company's annual cost per server at $2,200, so they set out to thin the herd.

Today, Delaware North has eliminated all but one of its six development servers and has chopped three production servers as well. At the same time, the company has improved availability of a crucial application from 80% to 98%. The key to the consolidation? Virtualization.

Virtual Reality

Server virtualization helps companies consolidate servers by allowing multiple instances of software, including operating systems, to run on the same box at the same time. Like Delaware North, most businesses run one application per server, which makes for a lot of unused processing power. In a mainframe environment, you have one or two big pieces of hardware, but in today's Unix or Windows environments, you have hundreds or even thousands.

Virtual machine software makes productive use of wasted horsepower, which means fewer servers overall. Virtualization software, such as VMWare, sits atop the operating system and creates an illusion of partitioned hardware. For example, you might install Windows Server 2003 as your server OS and then install VMWare atop it. With this done, you can install other Windows variants for testing or migration purposes and as many other applications as will fit on the hardware. The virtualization software creates a virtual server for each.

The concept of the virtual machine is not new; IBM mainframes used the technology extensively in the 1960s. But the buzz around virtualization today centers on Intel processor-based servers. This, after all, is where the low-hanging fruit is found. Almost every company in the world has underutilized server space and a network that connects this unused capacity. It's an extremely valuable resource that's going unused. One of the principles of the computer-powered software management model is to apply the best available technology to achieve the optimal solution; finding a way to use all that unharnessed server power is a situation calling out for a technology-based solution.

The Geeky Part

Sun Microsystems, HP, and IBM have all been driving initiatives to manage multiple computers more efficiently, capitalizing on that unused capacity. At Sun Microsystems, this technology is called N1. N1's concept is that it treats the disparate boxes in a customer's data center as one pool of resources. Just as a single server operating system in an individual server manages resources, schedules jobs, and deals with certain types of failures, N1 does this for many resources.

The difference is that, whereas a computer's operating system manages components such as microprocessors, memory, and disks, N1 manages the components of the network itself: servers, storage, firewalls, and load balancers. The idea is rather than dispatch a squadron of system administrators to manually swap out boxes, rewire connections, and load new software to respond to changes in the business, N1 manages all these as a pooled set of resources, adding and subtracting as necessary. This concept is similar to the virtual server solution discussed earlier, except on a much grander scale.

As a major producer of IT infrastructure, Sun has seen the data center grow in complexity. In the past, the service delivered to users was usually one piece of software on one box. Now the business service delivered is made up of many pieces of software running on many boxes, yet the operations and management capability has not scaled enough to keep it simple to manage.

Here are some of the challenges:

- The more services are scaled, the more complex and inefficient the operation and management of the system because each box or new software instance equals one more thing to manually install, configure, monitor, and change manage.

- Provisioning is usually for peak usage; however, peak usage rarely occurs, so it's inefficient and utilization is low.

- Moving things between silos is very difficult, so flexibility suffers.

- Inefficiency and lack of agility affect the capability to meet the quality-of-service needs of users.

If repurposing these resources were easy, these problems could be solved. Resources could be moved wherever and whenever necessary. Today that's a long and error-prone manual process, and that's where Sun's N1 comes in. By automating these tasks, resources can be repurposed and reallocated quickly, reliably, and repeatedly.

Scott McNealy, Sun's founder and CEO, describes N1 as what we think of as systems or servers, whether thin-node systems or fat-node SMPs like Sun's Sunfire 15K, become components in a new, larger metasystem. An N1 system can be a rack of blades or a Sunfire 15K, each of which can be its own domain or which can all be combined into a single domain. It's growing from a row of racks in a cluster to a large computer room full of heterogeneous servers and storage. The new system virtualizes at the network level, not just the single-box OS level. N1's goal is to manage applications not just on a server-by-server basis, but across the whole network.

The ability to add, remove, and reconfigure system resources without the attendant headaches of physical installations is good all by itself. The built-in redundancy, performance management, and fault-tolerance is key to the value of N1. Sun's N1 isn't the only system of its type; others are also pursuing their own vision of utility computing

What the Other Guys Are Up To

IBM's largest example to date of grid computing for an enterprise is the internal grid dubbed intraGrid. IBM's intraGrid, based on Globus, is a research and development grid that enables IBM to leverage many worldwide assets for research purposes, such as utilizing a grid to support distributed scalability testing.

HP has been a pioneer in grid computing since the early 1980s. In 1982, Joel Birnbaum, then head of HP Laboratories, described the notion of an "information utility." *Utility* here was meant as an analog to the more pedestrian utilities such as water, electricity, and so on. Part of Birnbaum's vision was that this *utility* was fully pervasive by encompassing all computers, automobiles, microwave ovens, and the like.

Planetary Scale Computing

HP Laboratories has built an entire lab around its vision of planetary scale computing. The effort seeks to design a robust infrastructure for the future, looking past current models for providing processing and data storage capacity. A new model is the target, one that can handle the next level of demand. Top-level objectives for third-generation systems include allocating resources wherever and whenever they're needed most, an infrastructure based on a shared pool of processing power, and data storage capacity that can be automatically reconfigured in minutes instead of days or weeks.

A first result of this effort is the Utility Data Center (UDC). The HP UDC is a solution that virtualizes all the resources in the data center—servers, networking, storage, and applications—and allows dynamic resource allocation and reallocation among applications, thereby making the IT infrastructure more adaptive.

Staunch believers in eating your own cooking, one of the early adopters of this technology was HP Labs itself. In moving to the UDC, HP Labs consolidated its distributed servers into two data centers— one in Palo Alto, California, and one in Bristol, England. These data centers run the core applications for HP Labs, such as email, Web serving, and library services. These data centers also serve as the computing platform for research conducted throughout HP Labs in areas as diverse as rich media, mobility, security, and fundamental science such as nanotechnology.

According to John Sontag, the program manager for the project, the UDC fills a number of needs for HP Labs. "Most importantly, it is our production facility, the place where we run all the services, that the HP Labs business uses on a daily basis," he says. "Secondly, it is where our researchers get access to servers, networking, and storage resources to perform their research. It's also a platform that will allow us to collaborate with other HP businesses."

Satisfying the global nature of these solutions, the UDC also is an infrastructure that lends itself to collaboration with customers and researchers outside HP. Examples include organizations such as the University of California, Berkeley; the University of Bristol; and the Gelato Federation, a worldwide consortium focused on enabling open-source computing solutions for research. One factor that enabled HP Labs to implement the UDC was the capability to pool the portion of the research budget allocated to the purchase of computer systems with the IT budget for running single solutions for many uses.

The installation of the UDC at HP Labs immediately provided numerous benefits, not the least of which was financial. "Installing the UDC is enabling us to quadruple the number of servers in our data centers in Palo Alto and Bristol while keeping our people and real-estate costs essentially flat," says Sontag. Although it sounds imposing, none of this hardware or software is particularly esoteric. The beauty of the UDC model is that it maximizes the benefits you can obtain through standardization.

Another example to illustrate the potential of grid computing is the BIRN project. Biomedical Informatics Research Network (BIRN) is studying brain imaging of human neurological disease and associated animal models. The effort is being carried out among 12 universities. In addition to using HP systems in this effort, BIRN has a large scientific instrument (an electron microscope) in Japan as part of its grid. This is a great example of virtual organizations collaborating, sharing data, and resources and linking in atypical resourses in a grid.

More important for the long-term, the large impact of grid computing is the commercial deployments. Gary Campbell, Senior Vice-President of Strategic Architecture in the Office of Corporate Strategy and Technology at HP says, "We are at the cusp of this taking place. When grid was united with Web services, the ability to address the needs and concerns of commercial applications was greatly increased. The next few years are a key time for grid. Early deployments, rapid learnings, improved robustness, and a greater range of applicability will all conspire to make grid a valuable and necessary tool and technology for the enterprise."

Query on Demand: Google

Few software applications require as much computation per request as Internet search engines. On average, a single query reads hundreds of megabytes of data and consumes tens of billions of CPU cycles. Supporting a peak request stream of thousands of queries per second requires a unique infrastructure.

Google's developers recognized from the beginning that providing the fastest, most accurate results required a new kind of server setup. Whereas most search engines ran off a handful of large servers that often slowed under peak loads, Google employed a grid of linked PCs to quickly find each query's answer. Today, for example, each time a consumer hits the infamous "Google Search" button, in just milliseconds, Google culls through 4.2+ billion Web pages to display the results. The innovation has paid off in faster response times, greater scalability and lower costs. It's an idea that others have since copied, while Google has continued to refine its back-end technology to make it even more efficient.

Operating thousands of linked PCs instead of a few high-end multiprocessor servers incurs significant management costs. However, for a relatively homogenous application like search, where most servers run one of very few applications, these costs can be managed through standardization (as we have seen) and automation. With automation, the time and cost to maintain 1,000 servers isn't much more than the cost of maintaining 100 servers because all the machines have identical configurations. Similarly, the cost of automated monitoring using a scalable application monitoring system does not increase greatly with grid size.

As the Internet grows, Google's challenges grow. However, being able to standardize and automate around a unique application has enabled Google to cost-effectively manage performance of what is arguably one of the largest computers in the world, while maintaining the high quality of service levels consumers expect.

Us, Too

Naturally, I'm going to tell you what Oracle is doing with grid technology, as well. Oracle has also been pursuing its unique vision of grid computing. An implementation of the Oracle E-Business Suite, while similar for enterprise customers, is not identical. Search applications and email applications can be architected for "the many" because the business process flows they automate are simple. However, this is not the case for process manufacturing. Tropicana's juice production process and Unocal's oil production process share some things in common but are far from identical. The fact that these applications are similar but not identical has driven many of our design decisions, just as the search application has driven Google's architecture.

Oracle's On Demand Grid serves several hundred enterprise customers and has been architected and running since early 2002. It is architected for thousands of servers and hundreds of terabytes of data. When a customer is first initialized, a slice of the grid is carved off for that customer's needs. As the customer progresses from initialization through implementation into production, grid control rules are established that allow the grid to respond to an increased need for CPUs or disks. CPU or disk resources are added as needed, on demand. If you apply this concept to our static call center example from the beginning of the chapter, you could imagine capacity expanding seamlessly as demand increases. No costly requirements analysis, downtime for upgrades, or offshore migration would be needed.

Oracle's grid technology enables the user to scale up when he needs it—closing books, Christmas shopping, or seasonal travel—and then scale down the demand when he doesn't need it. The computers monitor utilization and add Web, forms, or database tiers, which is a much more efficient way to use computing than the traditional model. Rather than attempting to size each customer uniquely, you can measure the overall utilization of the grid elements and do capacity planning based on historical data of the aggregate usage across hundreds of customers. This is similar to the way in which a public utility plans capacity, sizing for a large group of customers rather than for a single household.

Automatic Performance Management

As you've no doubt noticed by now, I keep coming back to the theme of automating repetitive processes. Grids like the ones we've been discussing can make lightning-fast adjustments to maintain performance levels automatically. When server utilization exceeds a preset threshold, the monitoring diagnostic software decides whether this is due to a runaway process or excessive load. If it is a runaway process, the process is automatically terminated.

On the other hand, if the high server utilization is due to excessive load, the monitoring software notifies the automated provisioning system. The provisioning system then allocates additional nodes out of the free pool and configures them appropriately. Finally, the provisioning system reconfigures the network and brings the node online. A grid system managed by humans trained to identify and respond to spikes and lulls in demand might realize some performance advantages, but nothing like you can get with automated processes. And if you're thinking about hard-wiring in a physical server when demand spikes, you might as well hang up your tool belt and go home.

As you will see in Chapter 5, "You Can Never Be Too Available," Oracle's primary grid is replicated in a secondary site for disaster recovery. Clearly with this capability, it won't be too long until several continental grids are established to allow workload to be located nearer to the user, minimizing network cost and performance. Not only will this allow for better performance management, but this infrastructure also can provide the backbone for cross-continent disaster recovery services.

Conclusion

The industry needs to continue to innovate ways to manage the performance of complex software systems. The end of traditional people-powered performance management is near. No longer is it good enough to have a couple of smart performance experts to tune and tweak the performance of mission-critical applications. Computers must be engaged to use internal data coming from these systems to automatically tune the systems for peak performance and maximum utilization. Whether called on-demand computing, cluster computing, grid computing, or utility computing, some of the largest technology companies in the world have invested and continue to invest in this new generation of solutions.

5

You Can Never Be Too Available

While managing performance is important and sometimes costly, managing the availability of complex computing environments can be the biggest headache for a CIO and the biggest challenge for technology companies. Modern businesses, dependent on computers, can lose as much as $10,000 per minute when their systems are not available to perform critical business functions. In today's competitive environment, the costs of downtime in terms of lost revenue; damage to customer relationships, image, and reputation; or lost productivity can have a significant impact on profits. A few days of downtime can threaten a business' existence. Even a few hours of downtime during peak periods for global companies in transaction-oriented industries such as financial services, manufacturing, or e-commerce can make the difference between profitability and viability.

Before discussing some of the technology-powered solutions to
the challenges of availability management, it's important to be
grounded both as consumers and producers of software and hardware in the problem. Building reliable bridges is still a challenge for
civil engineers, and it is no different for computer engineers. Modern
systems must survive not only physical hardware failure, but also
software design bugs, operator errors, environmental disasters, and
the need to change. Once you understand the problem, you'll see
how companies such as IBM, Tandem (now a part of HP), and Oracle
as well as university researchers at Stanford, the University of Illinois,
and Carnegie Mellon University are developing new ways to ensure
continuous availability.

Are You Saying That 99% Isn't Good Enough?

Yes. I'm saying that 99% reliability isn't good enough. Here's why:
Although measuring availability with a whole lot of 9s has been traditional, in reality the numbers all seem to blend together. 98%, 99%,
99.2%—they all seem more or less the same and all look pretty good.
Maybe it's because they would all be *A's* and most of us would have
been glad to get an *A* on any exam. If, instead, we consider that one
year contains more than 500,000 minutes (on a 24-hour clock), 98%
uptime means you're out of service for more than 10,000 minutes a
year—that's 167 hours, or almost 7 days! Even at 99%, you're out of
service for more than 5,000 minutes per year, or 3.5 days. Now 98%
and 99% availability don't sound so good. Furthermore, if you
consider the cost of a minute of outage at only $1,000 per outage
minute, the difference between 98% and 99% availability is $5 million
per year—not chump change.

Making Yourself More Available

Providing high availability is not easy. Leading analyst firms estimate that enterprises wanting to eliminate the majority of planned downtime will need to spend approximately 3.5 times the cost of a standard application. Even if this amount is spent, analysts estimate that only 20% of applicants will actually achieve 99.5% availability. Given that our goal is to surpass that 99.5% benchmark by a comfortable margin, the odds don't look very good.

There are two fundamental ways to reduce the number of outage minutes. First, you can increase the time between outages—often called the *mean time between failures (MTBF)*. Second, you can decrease the time to recover from the outage. Outages can be classified into five broad classes: physical, design, operations, environmental, and reconfiguration. Physical failure is the classic model of computer failure. Although physical hardware faults are not a dominant source of system failure, hardware faults do occur. Whether it's a disk failure or a power supply failure, physical faults are a side effect of any manufactured item. Design outages are the primary cause for software failures, although this class can apply to hardware as well. Operator-related outages account for human error, whereas environmental outages come from both unplanned sources such as earthquakes and planned terrorist actions. Reconfiguration is the final class of outages and accounts for the planned outages that always seem to occur in the middle of a crunch project.

Call the Exterminator

Design faults, which are the primary form of software failure, have plagued software designers from day one. Software bugs dominate, but most fault assessment techniques do not differentiate between permanent and transient failures in software. Bugs occurring in computer systems can be classified into two types: Heisenbugs and Bohrbugs.

The basis for these bug classifications is the ease with which the failure produced by the bug can be repeated. If a Bohrbug is present in the system, a failure always occurs when you repeat the operation that causes the failure. The *Bohrbug* was named after the Bohr atom: Just as the Bohr atom is solid, the Bohrbug is also solid and easily detectable by standard techniques. In the case of a Heisenbug, the error vanishes on a retry. The word *Heisenbug* comes from Heisenburg's Uncertainty Principle, which states that it is fundamentally impossible to determine the position and momentum of a particle at the same time. With bugs, it means sometimes the bug is there and sometimes it isn't. If we try to apply standard debugging techniques to a Heisenbug problem, we might find that the error has disappeared.

Most industry software systems are released only after design reviews, unit tests, system tests, alphas, betas, and even a few brave customer trials. They are mostly free of Bohrbugs, which are easily caught; it's the Heisenbugs that remain. Anyone who has used Ctrl+Alt+Delete to squash a Heisenbug in Windows understands the seemingly random nature of these problems. More importantly, as you sit waiting for your system to reboot—perhaps cycling through a Safe Mode restart and a recovery cycle—you know how frustrating the downtime can be. Applied to large systems, Heisenbugs can be quite costly.

Beyond the Bugs

Design faults are not the only source of downtime. Human operators can also be a significant contributor to system failure. In Jim Gray's book *Why Do Computers Stop and What Can Be Done About It?*, a study of more than 2,000 Tandem NonStop systems revealed that system administration, which includes operator actions, system configuration, and system maintenance, was the main source of failures at 42%. People make mistakes far more frequently than computers.

Systems can also fail from environmental faults. According to the National Power Laboratory, each year the typical computer location experiences 36 spikes, 392 voltage fluctuations, 128 voltage surges, and 15 blackouts. More than half of the service calls and downtime experienced on computers and networks can eventually be traced back to the utility power or mains. The Power Electronics Application Center estimates that damages annually add up to $26 billion in lost data, time, and damaged hardware due to power failures. According to estimates by the Electric Power Research Institute in Palo Alto, California, power outages cost U.S. businesses $29 billion annually.

While unplanned outages cause many failures on a 24/7 clock, planned outages are also a source of service downtime. A *planned outage* is defined as the period of time that software in the production environment is unavailable due to change management require-ments. Planned outages can affect customers individually or as a group and can include proactive software maintenance, customer-specific infrastructure upgrades, and relocation or reconfiguration of the customer's software environment.

There isn't any such thing as a perfect computer program or system, but Software on Demand can reduce downtime in a couple of ways. First, using the same availability management processes repetitively ensures higher quality. Second, by carefully standardizing the environment—ranging from eliminating unknown software to ensuring a clean power supply—they create fewer opportunities to accidentally introduce unanticipated conflicts. Finally, by freeing human operators from mundane tasks, the problems that do re-quire human intervention can be addressed immediately and appropriately.

DIAL TONE RELIABILITY

Most people consider the most reliable, available system in the world to be the U.S. telephone system. We often refer to *dial-tone reliability* to describe the highest level of availability. On April 6, 1992, the FCC required telephone service providers to begin reporting outages of 30 minutes or more that will potentially affect 50,000 customers. Recently, the standard has been raised to both report on outages affecting 30,000 customers as well as to report on any outages affecting major airports, 911, nuclear power plants, major military installations, and key government facilities, regardless of the number of customers/lines affected.

The results might surprise you. For the past 10 years, the data has been collected. These are the summary statistics:

YEAR	TOTAL NUMBER OF OUTAGES	MEAN TIME BETWEEN OUTAGES	MEDIAN DURATION OF OUTAGES
1993	157	2.32 days	2.56 hours
1994	160	2.28 days	2.5 hours
1995	169	2.16 days	3.72 hours
1996	174	2.10 days	2.93 hours
1997	105	1.07 days	3.38 hours
1998	181	2.02 days	2.98 hours
1999	176	2.07 days	2.62 hours
2000	184	1.99 days	2.32 hours
2001	154	2.37 days	3.06 hours
2002	117	3.12 days	3.42 hours
10-year average	166	2.24 days	2.94 hours

These outages were caused by everything from Heisenbugs to human error to heavy rain. These statistics suggest that, on average, the phone company always has someone somewhere without dial tone. Not to mention that your own personal service can be disrupted when your cat knocks the phone off your desk—a problem you might not discover for several hours while the outside world is unable to reach you. Applied to your customers, you'll probably agree that dial tone reliability isn't good enough.

The State of the Art

Many hardware and software solutions are competing to provide high-availability service. Tolerating failure has been an area that has received a lot of attention. In 1974, James G. Treybig and three former HP engineers founded Tandem Computers Incorporated, now the HP NonStop Enterprise Division, in Cupertino, California. Their vision was to build a machine with enough sophistication to withstand the loss of any single component—a computer with "no single point of failure."

NonStop technology created the infrastructure that has enabled customers all over the world to transform the way they process online transactions. The first NonStop server was designed to perform a critical task—fault-tolerant transaction processing. To achieve that objective, unique hardware and software was built. An amusing example occurred in 1989: During the Loma Prieta earthquake, Pacific Bell's NonStop servers physically fell over but continued operations without experiencing any downtime thanks to the NonStop architecture. Today much of the world's stock markets and ATM networks depend on NonStop technology.

IBM developed clustering technology as a means to attain high availability. S/390 clustering, called Parallel Sysplex technology, uses a form of clustering in which all servers appear to the business application as a single server. This form of clustering—known as *single system image*—enables Parallel Sysplex clusters to provide continuous availability by allowing workloads to be balanced across multiple servers. S/390 Parallel Sysplex clustering is the business solution for helping to ensure that applications are available through any downtime event and that revenues from sales and other business opportunities are not lost to the competition.

Recently, Oracle has used the real application cluster (RAC) to bring many of these basic principles to the world of Linux/Intel computing. RACs run on top of a hardware *cluster*, which is a group of independent servers, or nodes, that cooperate as a single system. The primary cluster components are processor nodes, a cluster interconnect, and a shared storage subsystem. The nodes share access to the storage subsystem and resources that manage data, but they do not physically share main memory in their respective nodes. A node can be made up of multiple processors, and a common type of node is a Symmetric Multi-Processor (SMP) node. Each node has its own dedicated system memory as well as its own operating system and database instance. Oracle's cluster database combines the memory in the individual nodes to provide a single view of the distributed cache memory for the entire database system. RAC technology is at the heart of the Oracle on Demand grid computer.

Technologies such as NonStop, Sysplex, and RAC end traditional availability management techniques by providing the capability to avoid the downtime that can be caused by any individual failure in a system. By rerouting traffic away from a damaged component or compromised system, the impact of any given fault can be minimized, giving the humans in the equation some time to address the fault and the problems causing it. Even with fault-tolerant systems, though, it's important to improve recovery time so that damaged systems can return to normal function as quickly as possible.

Recovery-Oriented Computing

The academic community has also focused on the challenges of providing high-availability computing. Armando Fox at Stanford University and Dave Patterson at the University of California Berkeley have been leading a research effort dubbed recovery-oriented computing (ROC). Patterson was a co-leader of the RISC architecture movement along with John Hennesey, now president of Stanford.

The work has focused on four key principles, the first of which is speedy recovery. Problems are going to occur, so we should design systems that recover quickly. Second, we must give operators better tools with which to pinpoint the sources of faults in multicomponent systems. Third, we must build systems that support an undo function, similar to those in word-processing programs, so operators can correct their mistakes. Finally, computer scientists should develop the ability to inject test errors; these would permit the evaluation of system behavior and assist in operator training.

Building for Recovery

The most common way to fix Web site faults or even Windows failures is to reboot the entire system, which takes anywhere from 10 seconds if the application alone is rebooted to a couple of minutes if the whole thing is restarted. The Stanford team is working on mechanisms to reduce the granularity of the reboot by micro-rebooting just the necessary subcomponents. With smaller components, the reboot takes much less time. So, instead of seeing an error message, a user would experience a 3-second delay followed by resumption of normal service.

To help analyze complex malfunctions in systems, the ROC team is building technology to determine which components are at fault. This technology is called PinPoint. Every time someone surfs to a PinPoint-enabled Web site, the program traces which software components participated in delivering service to that user. When a particular access request fails—for example, the user gets an error message from the site—PinPoint notes this fact. Over time, the monitoring application analyzes the mix of components that were activated in both failed and successful requests using standard data-mining techniques. By doing this, PinPoint can help find out which components are causing most of the failures. The additional information gathered by the failure-analysis code slows down the system by at most 10%. Unlike the traditional solution—which requires elaborate preplanning every time the software suite changes—PinPoint works with any combination of software components.

Brought out of the research community, predictable recovery of the database system is one of the most difficult operations to provide bounds on because database recovery cannot generally be interrupted without consequences and the amount of required resources is hard to predict. The need for recovery predictability has motivated Oracle to provide a special parameter. FAST START MTTR (mean time to recovery) TARGET allows an administrator to specify the average amount of time recovery should take.

Suit of Armor

At the University of Illinois Urbana-Champaign, researchers are also working on new technology to improve the availability of applications. The Adaptive Reconfigurable Mobile Objects of Reliability (ARMOR) project under the direction of Professor Ravi Iyer has been developing new approaches for designing and validating high-availability applications. The design techniques are centered on the use of ARMOR, which provides a wide range of detection and recovery services—a suit of armor. ARMOR services can be used to provide progressively higher degrees of availability for a user application.

Level 1 is completely transparent. It detects application process crashes, recovers the application by restarting, and migrates failed application processes to another node. Level 2 is an enhancement of standard system libraries and provides applications with the capability to reestablish broken TCP connections, duplicate file writes to protect data on disk, and message logging. Finally, Level 3 gives applications a data auditing framework, allows for check-pointing selected application states, and provides customized voting on application output.

Fixing the People

Research is also being done at Carnegie Mellon University under the direction of Roy Maxion to develop technology that might prevent operator/human-induced outages. His tool MetriStation provides an up-front measurement of the operator population to see which types of people and skills will be involved. In addition, it characterizes the specific elements of the tasks expected to be performed. The measurement will tell you where you went right and where you went wrong, and error analysis will lead you to the corrections that need to be made to the user interface.

It turns out that most operator error is due to forgetfulness, or errors of omission. Other operator errors are due to poor exception handling. Perhaps the person was too stressed to think of the right thing, or no one thought out in advance that certain conditions were likely to occur and put procedures in place to cover them. One excellent example is airport baggage handling: Say you are at the ticket counter. You've checked your bag and then notice that it's checked to the wrong destination. Can they get the bag back off the belt?

At least in the airports I've visited—and believe me, that's a lot of airports—there is no provision for getting that bag back in any easy way other than crawling out to the plane and getting it by hand. As it turns out, sending luggage to the wrong destination is a fairly common mistake, so you'd think the baggage system would have a way to recover from it.

Can I Have a Do-over?

The ability to undo an operation is also a fundamental area the Stanford and Berkeley team is working in. Undo also serves as a basic mechanism in any transaction processing system to ensure that an operation either completes or does not commit. To demonstrate a general approach, the Berkeley team is working on an undo capability for email systems. They have recently completed the prototype of an email system featuring an operator undo utility.

Suppose a virus infects a conventional email storage server. The system operator must disinfect the server, which is a laborious job. This system, however, records all the server's activities automatically, including discarded messages. If the system is infected, the operator could employ the undo command to turn back the clock to a safe point before the arrival of the virus. Software that attacks that virus could then be downloaded. Finally, the operator could play forward all the email messages created after the infection, returning the system to normal operation.

The newly installed antivirus software would filter all subsequent email traffic. In this way, the operator could undo the damage without losing important messages. To prevent potential confusion among users—who might notice that some emails had been eradicated—the system could send a message saying that notes were deleted during an attempt to stop the spread of a virus.

Error Injection

Finally, the ROC team is working on general mechanisms for fault injection. Fault injection has been a common method for verifying hardware reliability and testability but is only now being brought to software. A group of Berkeley graduate students has developed the Fig (for fault injection in glibc) to test the capability of programs to correctly cope with unexpected errors in the standard C library.

Error injection permits computer programmers to test their repair mechanisms, which is difficult to do. Fig would allow operators to try their hands at diagnosing and repairing failures, perhaps on a small experimental system if not on the real thing.

High Availability in Real Life

Although much work continues in the research community, the demands for high availability in commercial applications is not waiting. I'd like to return to an earlier example to show you how Oracle's On Demand services manage the need for high-availability systems.

The Software on Demand service provided by Oracle started on day one with 24/7 management of the applications, database, and systems in the default operational model. However, because we're working with global clients and because we, as humans, require sleep, we chose a model that allows continuous service with highly qualified humans in place during daylight hours regardless of the time zone. From centers located in North America, Europe, and Asia, Oracle manages 24/7—always using the center in daylight hours to provide prime-time management for the computers in that time zone.

So, whether it's a U.S. customer operating in Europe or an Asian customer operating in that region, the global infrastructure provides management all day, all night. The service is provided independently of the hardware's location. In the modern era of networking, the people using the system, the people managing the system, and the computers themselves do not have to be in the same physical location. A great example is the management of Pepsi-Tropicana's European IT operations.

Pepsi-Tropicana's end user is located in several countries in Europe: Belgium, Holland, UK, and France. However, the people managing the computers are located in the United States, Europe, and India. The computers are located in the middle of the United States, and the development organization that builds and supports the process manufacturing application is located in New York. The system is fault-resilient, highly available, and secure.

When the Unthinkable Happens

With the events of September 11 and the passage of Sarbanes-Oxley in the United States, the subject of disaster recovery has come front and center. Software on Demand solutions must include disaster recovery that is designed in—not added on. In late 2001, Oracle On Demand introduced a service that provides the ability to tolerate a complete site failure and recover in less than 2 hours with applications and data that are synchronized. The service uses state-of-the-art Oracle technology, in conjunction with proven availability management processes, to quickly recover from a disaster or unplanned outages.

One technology that makes such a recovery possible is application synchronization. *Application synchronization* ensures that a secondary site is regularly synchronized with the primary site and is maintained at the same patch and version level as those on the primary site. Oracle's application synchronization service is one of the few that can actually accomplish this task, although other solutions will become more prevalent.

Oracle's On Demand disaster recovery service also ensures operational readiness assurance by providing semiannual disaster rehearsal verification. Most CIOs recognize that few disaster recovery plans have ever been tested. That position, too, will undoubtedly change in the wake of recent events. The disaster recovery process begins with contacting the customer to discuss a failover or switch-over decision. After a mutual agreement to declare a switch-over is reached, a route change begins and sends business user network traffic to the Backup On Demand grid at the backup data center. Managed recovery of the standby database and application synchronization processes is initiated to bring the new system and applications into the grid management and monitoring framework. Ensuring a smooth cut-over is important, so baseline tests on the data integrity of the backup production environment are performed. The backup production environment is then activated, followed by notification of the customer.

With an increasing dependence on computers and increasing fear of terrorism, it will not be long before disaster recovery is considered as standard as RAID disks are today. Work continues in universities and corporations to develop ever-higher levels of availability in computing systems. But in the modern world, the greater concern and investment has shifted from protection against accidental failure to protection against deliberate attacks. Managing the security of computing environments has become front-page news for both our personal computers and the corporate computing environment.

6

Batten Down the Hatches

Quantifying the cost of security breaches is difficult because most companies do not report attacks. However, the annual Computer Security Institute and the U.S. Federal Bureau of Investigation computer crime and security survey tallied more than $201 million in quantified financial losses in 2003. Among respondents, the most frequently cited forms of attack were viruses (82%) and insider abuse of network access (80%). Theft of proprietary information was the greatest source of financial loss. Total losses amounted to $70 million with an average reported loss of $2.7 million. In a shift from previous years, the second most expensive computer crime among survey respondents was denial of service, with a cost of $65,643,300. The complete 2003 CSI/FBI Computer Crime and Security Survey is available at **www.gocsi.com**.

These are uncertain times. Reports of cyber attacks are dramatically on the rise, and many companies are unprepared to detect and deal with an attack should one occur. Additionally, the costs associated with a security threat can be prohibitive, with Gartner estimating that the cost of fixing a security problem reactively is 50% more than the cost of managing the security proactively (**http://www2.cio.com/metrics/2002/metric364.html**). The costs of security keep rising each year. Recently, Bull and IDC completed a survey. The white paper prepared by IDC France analyst Eric Ochs states that, in Europe during 2002, IT security investments (hardware, software, and services) totaled $5 billion, up 25% from their 2001 level. These security investments accounted for an average of 1.8% of overall IT investments in Europe in 2002. However, with companies being more security aware, their spending was nearly 5% of their IT budgets.

A Reason to Lose Sleep

Whether managed in-house, or externally through service providers, security concerns keep CEOs up at night. Providing security management is not easy. Gartner believes that through 2005, one in five enterprises will experience a serious attack that causes a material loss (**http://www2.cio.com/metrics/2002/metric364.html**). Repairing that damage will exceed the cost of prevention measures by 50%— not to mention the damage done to the reputation of the victim. A startling 90% of these attacks will exploit known security flaws for which a patch is already available, a statistic that illustrates a serious lack of software security management. Why? Companies often wait too long to install patches on their systems or have difficulty adding patches because of testing procedures required in their computing environments.

The consequences of security attacks can be severe, resulting in damaged data and assets, business interruption, and infiltration and access to confidential and classified resources. After a computer is infiltrated, applying the security patch is no longer a sufficient remedy to guarantee its security. Successfully recovering from an attack can require the complete reinstallation of *every* compromised asset.

Many books have been and will be written on security management, but it is important to understand what some of the key technology areas are as we move from people-powered to computer-powered security management. Probably more than any of the other five areas, Software on Demand must remove people from the equation because they're always the largest security risk.

The fundamentals begin with authenticating users of the applications and the administrators of those systems, authorizing users for certain levels of access, and auditing the processes. These steps are important to enable a software on demand model to work for modern enterprises. We'll discuss a few examples from Oracle's On Demand business. We'll also go beyond the conventional and necessary security management processes to explore some of the advanced technologies on the border between availability and security (after all, whether you're protecting against a bomb or an earthquake, the computer has no way to know). Finally, we'll go inside one of the nation's leading research institutes and take a look into what the future holds for automating software security management.

Where to Start?

Security management starts with physical security. As discussed previously, the physical perimeter of the data facilities used by Oracle can withstand a semi-trailer truck hitting the exterior wall at 60mph. Armed guards patrol the premise, and 50 onsite cameras constantly record movements around the facility. Entry to the facility is through a weight-sensored mantrap with biometric hand scanners that ensure entry of only authorized personnel, one at a time.

A secure physical facility can be the first step for security management, but once outside the four walls of the data center, you can no longer provide physical security—short of building a bank vault around every component of your entire network. The industry solution to this challenge is to use encryption technology to ensure that, even if an attacker were able to physically compromise the network, the data would be unusable.

Virtually Private

Fortunately, virtual private networks (VPNs) can be extremely secure, even though they use physically insecure networks or even public networks. VPNs have proven popular because they offer operational savings while maintaining the security associated with private network infrastructure. Using a VPN, a traveling worker or branch office can be connected to the corporate network with a local phone call, providing significant savings over using long distance, 800 numbers, or leased lines. Security is maintained because the VPN uses a secure tunneled connection, allowing only authenticated users access to the corporate intranet. VPN solutions offer 128-bit encryption within the United States, with 40-bit encryption supported overseas where permitted by law.

A *VPN* can be described as the capability to tunnel through the Internet or other public network in a manner that provides the same security and other features formerly available only on private networks. With tunneling, a message packet is encapsulated within an IP packet for transmission across the public network, with the encapsulating information being stripped off upon arrival at the target network, such as the corporate local area network (LAN).

Know Thyself—and Thy People

A basic security requirement is that you know your users: You must first identify users before you can determine their privileges and access rights. Users can be authenticated in a number of ways before they are allowed to create a database session, for example. In database authentication, you can define users such that the database performs both identification and authentication of users. In external authentication, you can define users such that authentication is performed by the operating system or network service. Alternatively, you can define users to be authenticated by the Secure Sockets Layer (SSL).

As the world's largest producer of hops and hops products, John I. Haas, Inc., is an acknowledged industry leader. Because Haas operates in the time-sensitive and market-driven agriculture sector, improvements in operational efficiency have a marked effect on the bottom line. Haas has been a long-time user of Oracle's On Demand services and an early adopter of the SSL technology to provide secure access to Haas employees on a global basis. Haas stays competitive by effectively leveraging its internal business processes, thereby minimizing the resources needed to coordinate a large array of supplier goods and services and deliver world-class products.

To build on its strong base and foster future growth, Haas knew it had to revolutionize its IT infrastructure and operate more efficiently and strategically. At the same time, Haas wanted to avoid increasing its expenditure on IT resources. By allowing Oracle to provide its 11*i* applications online, Haas was able to redeploy some of its dedicated internal IT employees—a 28% shift. Haas was also able to avoid purchasing additional hardware. These increased efficiencies have netted Haas an annual operating savings of $180,000 and approximately $150,000 in asset productivity. Haas began the move to Oracle

On Demand in 2000 by focusing first on applications. Since then it has expanded its footprint and uses Technology On Demand services to drive corporate portals as well as Collaboration Suite On Demand to replace Exchange with a centrally managed, secure, low-cost email and file-sharing system.

Password, Please

Passwords are one of the basic forms of authentication. A user must provide the correct password when establishing a connection to prevent unauthorized use of the database. In this way, users attempting to connect to a database can be authenticated by using information stored in that database. Passwords are assigned when users are created. A database can store a user's password in the data dictionary in an encrypted format, and users can change their passwords at any time.

Having a central facility authenticate all members of the network clients to servers, servers to servers, and users to both clients and servers—is an effective way to address the threat of network nodes falsifying their identities. Strong authentication can also be established by using two-factor authentication: the combination of something a user knows, such as a PIN, and something the user has, such as a token card. Intranet users are commonly required to use a separate password to authenticate themselves to servers they need to access in the course of their work.

Multiple passwords, however, present several problems. Users have difficulty keeping track of different passwords, tend to choose poor ones, and tend to record them in obvious places. Administrators must keep track of a separate password database on each server and must address potential security problems arising from the fact that passwords are routinely and frequently sent over the network.

Oracle has pioneered single sign-on to do away with these problems. It enables users to log in to different servers using a single password to obtain authenticated access to all servers they are authorized to access. In addition, it simplifies the management of user accounts and passwords for system administrators.

Security As Policy

Confidentiality, integrity, and availability are the hallmarks of database security. Who should have the right to access data? What portion of all the data should a particular user be able to access? Which operations should an authorized user be able to perform on the data? Can authorized users access valid data when necessary?

Authorization is permission given to a user, program, or process to access an object or set of objects. The type of data access granted to a user can be read-only, or read and write. *Privileges* specify the type of data manipulation language (DML) operations upon which the user can perform data changes.

Any security policy must maintain a record of system activity to ensure that users are held accountable for their actions. Auditing helps deter unauthorized user behavior, which might not otherwise be prevented. It is particularly useful to ensure that authorized system users do not abuse their privileges. Fine-grained auditing can serve as an early warning system of users misusing data access privileges as well as an intrusion detection system for the database itself.

A strong audit facility allows businesses to audit database activity by statement, by use of system privilege, by object, or by user. You can audit activity as general as all user connections to the database and as specific as a particular user creating a table. You can also audit only successful operations or only unsuccessful operations. For example, auditing unsuccessful **SELECT** statements can catch users on fishing expeditions for data they are not privileged to see. Audit trail records can be stored in a database, making the information available for viewing through ad-hoc queries or any appropriate application or tool, or combined with operating system audit trails on selected operating systems, for ease of management.

Computer-powered auditing can be effective if established correctly. Auditing should be implemented within the server itself, not in a separate, add-on server that might be remotely situated from the statements being executed, thereby incurring network overhead. The granularity and scope of these audit options enable businesses to record and monitor specific database activity without incurring the performance overhead that more general auditing entails. By setting just the options you need, you should be able to avoid catchall and throwaway audit methods that intercept and log all statements and then filter them to retrieve the ones of interest.

Audit Planning

Good IT management requires regular independent security audits of the operations. SAS 70 Type 1 and Type 2 audits are recognized standards in the industry. Developed by the American Institute of Certified Public Accountants (AICPA) and launched in 1992, the internationally recognized Statement on Auditing Standards (SAS) No. 70 provides an independent verification of the descriptions of a service provider's control activities and processes.

A SAS 70 audit is particularly useful for companies that outsource the management of certain parts of their operations and need to undergo annual financial audits. They can show their auditor the SAS 70 report of their service suppliers so the auditor doesn't need to do annual financial audits. They can also show their auditor the SAS 70 report of their service suppliers so the auditor doesn't need to conduct its own audit of the provider's facility. Generally, the controls or processes audited are those that protect customer data, which usually includes the IT functions. Because of this, SAS 70 is generating a resurgence of interest from businesses that are required to meet new regulations designed to protect sensitive data.

A service provider must engage an independent accounting and auditing firm to conduct a review of the service in accordance with the standards defined in SAS 70. Following completion of the review, a formal report is issued that includes the auditor's assessment of service controls and processes at the period of time assessed by the auditor.

Specialized audits might also be required. In early 2000, The Bank of Montreal chose to use the Oracle E-Business Suite to reengineer the methodologies used to purchase $1.2 billion worth of goods and services each year and significantly reduce procurement spending. The Bank of Montreal has used automation to standardize purchase processes, eliminate unnecessary approvals or redundant transfers, and eliminate inefficient manual processes, thereby reducing the length of the purchasing cycle. Using a standard browser, employees have instant access to catalogs from which to procure items quickly, efficiently, and in line with the bank's established business rules and pricing policies.

These business benefits drove the bank to consider Oracle software, but it also was eager to focus on the purchasing process and not on buying computers and managing software. Consequently, they chose to have their applications delivered On Demand. With the computers located in the United States, the bank's auditors requested and were granted a special audit to ensure that adequate protection was in place.

The Next Big Thing

The same advances in technology that have made higher levels of performance and availability possible have created new and more dangerous threats to system security. The next generation of security management will need to provide another level of service to keep up with these increased threats. Some of this, again, is about policy and procedure—or effectively executing the established policy. For example, although patches were available from Microsoft for the SoBig, Blaster, and XYZ bugs, in almost all cases the patches were never applied to production systems. The key security management process called "from development to deployment" will need to become standard practice regardless of whether operations are outsourced.

Steve Printz, CIO at Pella, has made the practice of managing security patches in Microsoft software part of the underlying infrastructure. Rather than hope that individual users will ensure the security of their PCs, Pella HQ uses SMS technology. Using SMS enables individual systems to be managed and updated centrally and provides a rigorous change management process to guarantee a fixed period of time between the release of a security patch from Microsoft until it is on all 1,000+ Pella PCs. Of course, to do this Printz had to standardize all the PCs so he could define a security management process that could be repeated and ultimately automated. "We couldn't do it any other way. If we let each environment be different, the cost of managing would have been prohibitive, not to mention probably infeasible," he said.

Availability Meets Security

So, what's beyond? Automated security management will integrate technology from the world of high availability and introduce these innovations to the world of high security. High-availability technology has been developed over the years to protect against unintentional faults—physical failure, design faults, software bugs, environmental conditions, and operator error. Typically, security management is applied to protect against intentional faults: The human intended to compromise the system. The bomb was intended to destroy the computer. The software bug was intended to cause harm to the computer. Even though we might make a huge distinction between intended and unintended security threats, the computer doesn't really understand intent. In reality, what's the difference between a denial-of-service attack and a runaway process that consumes all the CPU resources?

In the physical world, the telcos have specified the Network Equipment and Building Standards (NEBS) that set conformance requirements to regulate the quality and reliability of equipment used throughout the telecom industry. One example is that the equipment must be capable of operating in a zone 4 earthquake area, meaning it must be capable of tolerating the shaking from an 8.3 Richter trembler. Recently, a large non-telecom commercial UK corporation with operations in London was interested in this technology—not because London is in earthquake country, but because this equipment is well-suited to handling a terrorist attack.

Trustworthy Computing

Security management, more than any of the other four key management areas, is a cross-disciplinary challenge. Issues of privacy, confidentiality, and security cross technology, public policy, and corporate policy boundaries. Given the cross-disciplinary issues of developing architectures and technologies for dramatically more secure networks and systems, the University of Illinois at Urbana-Champaign has launched the Center for Trustworthy Networked Systems (CTNS). CTNS is a multidisciplinary research and education center dedicated to creating networked information systems that offer the degree of trust needed for them to be relied on in the critical roles they play in our daily lives.

CTNS brings together more than 90 faculty, researchers, and students with expertise spanning networking and communications; computing and data storage; control, cryptography, and information hiding; simulation, analysis, experimentation, and system assurance; power, aerospace, and aeronautical systems; and economic, ethical, and legal issues.

CTNS is bringing together the significant research resources of several laboratories within the university. These include the Coordinated Science Lab, the Beckman Institute, and the Siebel Center. The Coordinated Science Lab, which recently marked its 50th anniversary, is one of the oldest research facilities in the nation. The Beckman Institute for Advanced Science and Technology was conceived early in 1983, when campus administrators decided to assemble a proposal for a unique new venture in multidisciplinary research at the university. Two faculty committees were subsequently appointed to develop plans for interdisciplinary research thrusts in the engineering and physical sciences and in the life and behavioral sciences.

The resulting committee reports formed the basis of a proposal submitted to Dr. Arnold O. Beckman in the fall of 1984. Dr. and Mrs. Beckman's gift of $40 million was announced in October 1985. The Beckman Institute is a multidisciplinary research center focusing on biological intelligence, human-computer intelligent interaction, and molecular and electronic nanostructures. Finally, one of the newest additions is the Siebel Center for Computer Science, a cutting-edge, twenty-first-century smart building, incorporating the newest innovations in mobile computing, distributed collaboration, and intelligent interaction.

One of the examples of a major research project underway at the university is under the direction of Professor Wen-mei Hwu, holder of the Jerry Sanders-AMD Endowed Chair in Electrical and Computer Engineering. The IMPACT project explores deep program analysis with secure computing as one of its major applications.

Secure utility computing simultaneously presents new opportunities and grand challenges for future compilers. On the one hand, utility computing combines application and platform software in a vertically integrated environment. Because the application and the operating system services can then be customized for each other, compilers can analyze and optimize across software boundaries that couldn't be crossed in most other environments. On the other hand, the economics of utility computing are demanding more compiler support for fault isolation, debugging, and energy efficiency.

The University of Illinois work is based on the premise that this in-depth analysis of software programs will make possible the development of revolutionary tools for detection, isolation, and correction of software errors both unintentional and intentional. The deep analysis information can also be used to craft operating system services into application containers that provide highly customized, secure, supportable, and efficient services to each application.

Traditional program analysis algorithms in modern compilers have been extremely limited in their capability to deal with memory references. This is one of the classic unintentional software failure modes as well as one of the classic intentional security holes. For example, accurate pointer analysis in large C programs remains a major challenge in computer science. As a result, compilers have been handicapped in their ability to offer useful information on memory references. Recently, a number of breakthroughs has occurred in the scalability of pointer analysis. As a result, Microsoft product teams now can run pointer analysis on their production code on a regular basis.

However, in existing analyses, scalability usually comes with a substantial amount of loss in accuracy. Such a loss can be tolerable in certain cases—for instance, instruction scheduling in optimizing compilers. However, when targeting more aggressive applications, such as fault detection/isolation for utility computing, accuracy can make a large difference. It is particularly so when programmers need to go through a filtering process for false positives caused by inaccurate analysis information.

To solve this problem, the IMPACT team has prototyped a new pointer analysis algorithm that achieves scalability with a much higher degree of accuracy, particularly for modern programs with complex call graphs. Their solution is based on properly confining information propagation throughout the analysis. This confinement, plus a novel approach to calculation of the final analysis information, achieves near linear growth in problem size as the program size grows. This enables their new algorithm to perform extremely accurate, or deep, pointer analysis on large, complex programs. A potential application of accurate pointer analysis information is the isolation of those program segments that could be the culprits in a detected memory corruption. Such accurate analysis information can greatly reduce the effort required to identify and remove the cause of software failures in a utility computing environment. Moreover, the analysis can also help identify other program segments that might have similar defects.

Deep program analysis doesn't end with accurate pointer analysis. Memory data flow analysis, which builds on accurate pointer analysis, identifies the information flow between program components via memory locations. Program logic analysis derives the logical formulation of program components and makes it possible to collapse and simplify program components.

These types of analysis have generally been considered intractable for large programs. However, it is clear that, although human software inspection can achieve a level of trust in a piece of software, we must use computers instead of people if we hope to achieve any consistency and accuracy in ensuring the security of large, complex programs. The University of Illinois IMPACT team remains convinced that they will develop algorithms to efficiently handle very large programs—that is, algorithms that control the problem size while achieving high accuracy.

Sometimes It's Just Personal

The application of increasing levels of technology to the challenges of building secure computing environments is worthwhile, but it should be noted that the protection of sensitive information, systems, or business is not always a technical problem. In a recent meeting between Oracle and the CIO of a major Asian bank, the CIO said, "I want you to take my HR and payroll data." Having never been asked this so directly, we asked him why. His response was, "I know my DBAs can see their salary, their boss's salary, and their peer's salary. I know your guys can see it as well, but why would they care?"

Conclusion

Security management is a complex mixture of people, processes, and policy. In a post-September 11 world, security management of information systems—both corporate and government—will only grow in importance. Security management, more than any of the other five disciplines, requires a move away from people-powered software management toward computer-powered software management because people have been and continue to be the biggest source of risk.

7

No Problem, No Worries

The National Institute of Standards and Technology (NIST) recently estimated that software bugs and errors cost the U.S. economy $59.5 billion annually. A report titled "The Economic Impacts of Inadequate Infrastructure for Software Testing" was commissioned by the NIST, a non-regulatory agency of the U.S. Department of Commerce's Technology Administration, which develops and promotes measurement, standards, and technology. According to the study, software developers already spend approximately 80% of development costs on identifying and correcting defects. However, despite these efforts, more than half of all errors are found downstream in the development process or during post-sale use. This dramatically impacts the cost of software sales and software support. Clearly, we need to change the way we manage problems today.

The Impact of Bugs

Software failures have become a main cause of system unavailability. Jim Gray's 1990 analysis of actual system performance, titled "A

Census of Tandem System Availability Between 1985 and 1990," showed that in the 5-year period from 1985 to 1990, the main cause of outage shifted from hardware to software. In that period, outages attributed to software grew from 33% to 60% as the major source of failure. The trend has continued, given the rise in installed lines of code, dependency between vendor software, and increased performance demands.

People-powered problem management has been honed for years. The right person shows up and hits a few magic keys, and the problem goes away. But just as with security management, we must move beyond a people-powered model to computer-powered problem management. In this chapter, we will start from the beginning—the software development process. One particular people-powered process that has demonstrated success is simple proofreading of software, also known as *software inspection*.

Although using people to do this is effective, a step beyond is to use computers to inspect software. Pioneering work at the University of Texas and Microsoft leverages research work that has been done in testing complex hardware configurations. Beyond the development of software and into deployment, we will show some of the standardizations and engineering practices we've used in Oracle's On Demand services to engineer for problem management by segregating customizations to a software product—often the largest source of problems in enterprise software.

But standardization is only the first step; ultimately problem management and problem resolution processes must be completely revamped in a world in which the software author also delivers the software. Rather than having a long, complex supply chain between the user of the software and the provider, a software-on-demand model compresses and collapses the supply chain between the user and provider, ultimately delivering better problem management and ending today's disconnected people-powered model.

Fixing the Process

As we have said, problem management is best dealt with at the source—the software development process. IBM pioneered a key people-powered process called software inspections in the 1970s. In many software development organizations, the process of reviewing or inspecting software is now required for all major changes or additions to the code base. Similar to the notion of proofreading in the writing or publishing business, there is ample evidence that manual peer review of software can lead to higher-quality software.

The cost of performing software inspection includes the individual preparation effort of each participant before the session and the effort of participants in the inspection session. Typically, four or five people participate and spend 1–2 hours of preparation and 1–2 hours of conduct each. This cost of 10–20 hours of total effort per session results in the early detection of 5–10 defects in 250–500 lines of new development code or 1,000–1,500 lines of legacy code. (O'Neill, Don. "National Software Quality Experiment: Results 1992–1999." Software Technology Conference, Salt Lake City, 1995, 1996, and 2000)

Another initiative focused on process improvement is the Software Engineering Institute's Capability Maturity Model (SEI-CMM) for software, as mentioned earlier. Some companies have made a major commitment to this form of process engineering. Since 1997, more than 1,000 software organizations have submitted assessment results to the SEI database with more than 70 publicly announcing their Level 5 ratings, as published on the SEI Web site.

The SEI has also focused on individual software developers and released the Personal Software Process (PSP). The PSP helps individual engineers improve their performance by bringing discipline to the way they develop software. Based on the practices found in the

CMM, the PSP can be used by engineers as a guide to a disciplined and structured approach to developing software.

Assisting Technology

However, process alone is not enough; technology must also contribute. At the dawn of the computer age, programmers had a hard time coaxing computers to tell them much about the programs they ran. Programmers were forced to invent different ways to obtain information about the programs they used. Eventually, programmers began to detect bugs by putting print instructions and other similar constructs inside their programs. By doing this, programmers were able to trace the program path and the values of key variables.

Although print statements were an improvement in debugging techniques, they still required a considerable amount of programmer time and effort. Programmers therefore needed a tool that could execute one instruction of a program at a time and print the value of any variable in the program. This would free the programmer from having to decide ahead of time where to put print statements because it would be done as he stepped through the program. Thus, runtime debuggers were born, enabling programmers to trace the program path and the variables without having to manually update their code. Today, virtually every compiler on the market comes with a runtime debugger.

Compiler technology continues to evolve. Static code analysis holds promise as a way to use technology to discover defects. Microsoft recently purchased a company focused on the business of building this form of technology. Static code analysis looks at data paths and uses symbolic path execution to detect certain classes of defects. The challenge, as we've discussed, is computational. Today, many programs tip the scales at over one million lines of code. Static analysis is computer intensive and can generate numerous false positives; therefore, it is used sparingly, and only as part of the code check process.

The Holy Grail has been to devise ways to prove the correctness of software. In a speech to the 17th Annual ACM Conference on Object-Oriented Programming, Systems, Languages and Application, Bill Gates said, "What is the state-of-the-art in terms of being able to prove programs, prove that a program behaves in a certain way? When I dropped out of Harvard, this was an interesting problem that was being worked on, and actually at the time I thought, 'Well, if I go and start a company, it will be too bad. I'll miss some of the big breakthroughs in proving software programs because I'll be off writing payroll checks.' And it turns out I didn't miss all that much in terms of rapid progress, which now has become, I'd say, in a sense, a very urgent problem."

Some possible directions include the use of powerful abstractions to reduce complexity and the use of more natural specification languages because they would be embraced by programmers. Such techniques are successfully being applied to complex hardware designs. Intel, IBM, and many others all have formal verification groups working on the problem. Jacob Abraham, a professor at the University of Texas, has shown that program-slicing techniques can be used to abstract hardware designs at the register-transfer level. *Program slicing* is a static program analysis technique that extracts the appropriate portions of programs relevant to an application; it has been applied to software debugging, testing, maintenance, and reuse. Application–to–large-benchmark circuits show a significant reduction in the size of the design to be analyzed for formally checking the correctness of a given property.

Abraham has also developed a novel approach for formally verifying software designs using sequential automatic test pattern generation (ATPG) tools developed for testing chips after manufacture. The properties are automatically mapped into a monitor circuit with a target fault so that finding a test for the fault corresponds to formally establishing the property. He has shown that combining program slicing with ATPG techniques reduces, by orders of magnitude, the time to formally check whether a software program is correct.

Just Try It

Finally, there is software testing. At a commercial software company, an equal amount of time is spent testing as is spent developing. Some software companies have as many testers as developers. In many cases, 50% of the developer's time is spent testing, so the ratio could be even more sharply slanted. Test cases are unbelievably expensive. In fact, there are often more lines of code in the testing systems— which, by the way, also need to be tested—than in the program itself. Sometimes it feels like software companies are less in the software industry than in the testing industry.

Does It Work?

The frustrating reality is that after the software reaches the customer, he often questions whether any time was spent ensuring the quality of the software product. With the spate of security defects in Microsoft software, customers again are saying that they could not tolerate this level of product quality in any other industry. But part of the problem is that software development does not end with the software company. In many cases, purchasing the software is only the beginning of the journey.

Customers end up customizing their enterprise software to fill gaps in the functionality, to adapt to a specific industry or legal requirement, or simply because the users want the software to act differently from how it does out of the box. It's not that customizations represent a failure—they are often legitimate and can even add a bit of competitive advantage to an otherwise vanilla software application. But companies tend to forget that they are not really in the software development business.

That's why some CIOs see upgrades as a prime opportunity to flush custom code from the system and replace it with a standard software program or interface from a vendor. Removing custom code makes upgrading easier because you don't have to rewrite the code each time a new enterprise version is released. It also makes integrating the software with other software systems inside the company easier. Let's look at a handful of examples.

Working It Out

During recent upgrades to KeySpan's Oracle E-Business Suite, KeySpan identified all the customized components of the software and the opportunities to switch to standard functions in the package's new version. KeySpan met with users to see which customizations they were willing to give up. When the two groups disagreed, they brought the discussion before a steering committee composed of functional and business leaders from across KeySpan.

Any customization resulted in one of two options: modifying the actual ERP code of the new version (which is both expensive and difficult) or adding a custom program outside of the ERP system to perform the function. That helped users understand just how much effort IT had to put into writing and maintaining those customizations. However, the users also had to do some research before they could appear before the steering committee to plead their case. They had to come up with a "no-technology" option that usually involved a change to the business process to fit with the software out of the box.

Moving Quickly

Empirix, a spinoff of Teradyne, had similar experiences. Founded in September 2000, Empirix combines the Web test and monitoring capabilities of RSW Software with the voice and network test capabilities of Hammer Technologies—both previously acquired by Teradyne. Empirix offers testing solutions for communications equipment manufacturers, e-businesses, and enterprise call centers, and it serves 2,000 customers worldwide.

Empirix had to have a solution in place by January 1, 2001, or pay significant chargeback fees to its former parent. The prospect of these charges was a positive motivator for Empirix to move rapidly. CIO Brenda Boyle, with the support of the CEO, made every choice to create a customization, a business decision. "Sometimes the users had valid reasons for wanting the customizations," Boyle says. "But we found nine and a half times out of 10 we could change the way we did business because, at the end of the day, it wasn't that critical; it was more a habit of how people were used to working."

The steering committee did not approve any customizations because they were invariably more expensive than the no-technology options. "When someone from the functional team came to them and said, 'We need the customization because we need to execute our process this particular way,' the committee would say, 'No you don't. You need to change your process. We'd rather invest this money in business.'"

In the end, Empirix went live on an enterprise application from Oracle in just 87 days. By calculating the disparity between startup costs in a conventional implementation and those with Oracle On Demand services, Boyle estimates the solution paid for itself in only seven months. Moreover, the solution provides for much higher levels of service than Empirix could provide itself.

Back to the Bugs

Much enterprise software changes so rapidly from its first release that CIOs wind up installing the upgrade all over again when the vendor finally comes out with a point release to fix the initial bugs.

Even though customizations and extensions to enterprise software will always be a part of the equation, we need a way to ensure that these pieces of software are identified, controlled, and maintained. Oracle identified the pain that CIOs and their respective organizations were feeling from the varying approaches to customization and turned this business problem into an engineering opportunity. After much research across industries and key system implementation partners, Oracle identified a framework that standardizes all requested customizations for its software.

CEMLI

The Customization, Extension, Modification, Localization, and Integration (CEMLI) framework was established by Oracle On Demand to categorize customizations, meaning software that had to be added by the customer or implementer to the Oracle applications.

Approximately 20 classes comprise the CEMLI framework. A classic example of software that must be added to the system unique to a specific application is a localization. *Localizations* are country-specific requirements—statutory and country-specific business practices—that are not included in the standard software package.

Oracle has researched and established a series of known localizations. These include, for example, the integrated receiving, cash management, and period average costing functions that might be required in Brazil. As with all CEMLIs, the management of localizations requires additional people-powered management, dependent on the degree of the CEMLI. Other CEMLI classes include reports, forms, SQL scripts, and workflows.

Now, for the first time, anyone can identify customization requirements and establish a price for managing these unique pieces of software. No longer is customization of software "good" or "bad"—it only has a cost. We have had some experiences in which the cost to manage the CEMLIs is larger than managing the entire Oracle application. Now the CIO can ask the business whether it wants to spend x amount of dollars for the uniqueness or whether it can use the standard product and save money.

This is no different from the physical world, where standard products such as Toyota Corollas are cheaper (and have higher reliability) than custom-crafted cars such as McLaren F1s (which cost $1 million and are less reliable). The cost of servicing the one is many times the cost of servicing the many. Today's On Demand customers have anywhere from 0 to more than 1,000 CEMLIs. By creating the CEMLI framework, customers have the flexibility to extend applications in a standard engineered environment and make the business tradeoffs.

It's Still Not Going to Be Perfect

Although being able to engineer a solution that isolates, compartmentalizes, and controls software goes a long way toward creating cleaner change, in the end to err is human and problems will surface in the field. It is left to problem management processes to rationalize these. Problem management is typically performed in five steps: problem determination, diagnosis, bypass and recovery, problem resolution, and problem tracking and control.

Problem determination consists of detecting a problem and completing the steps necessary for beginning problem diagnosis, such as isolating the problem to a particular subsystem. *Problem diagnosis* consists of determining the precise cause of the problem and the action required to solve it. *Problem bypass and recovery* consists of attempts to bypass the problem, either partially or completely. It provides only a temporary solution and relies on problem resolution to permanently solve the problem. *Problem resolution* consists of efforts to eliminate the problem. It usually begins after problem diagnosis is complete and often involves corrective action, such as replacing failed hardware or software. *Problem tracking and control* consists of tracking each problem until a final resolution is reached. Vital information describing the problem is recorded in the problem database.

In a traditional world, problem management is intrinsically difficult. Software development and support is treated as a different entity from internal customer support and operations. When a problem arises and is reported to the software vendor, the vendor usually has to perform the time-consuming step of replicating a problem on its side, which can entail the transfer of log and trace files and a lot of frustration on both sides.

Traditional problem management is similar to an episode of *Car Talk* on NPR. A user calls with a car problem. One of the Clappet brothers asks a leading question, and then they begin to make jokes as they try to diagnose the problem over the phone. We all find this amusing, but software problem management is much the same— only the jokes aren't as good.

Furthermore, in the traditional model, service is reactive. The software vendor might know about a problem that affects other customers, but because the vendor has no direct contact with customers' systems, it can't proactively apply a patch. Instead, it waits for the customer to log a support issue, which usually happens only when the problem impacts one or more systems. According to Thomas Sweeney, president of the Service and Support Professionals Association, "There is a large impact of slow problem resolution. Year over year, the number-one complaint from customers [about software vendors] is the time to resolve issues." Having a complete picture of the systems allows the software company to perform proactive problem management. At Oracle On Demand, we catalog all the problems in a single database, proactively search the database, focus on root cause analysis, and apply a fix-once-apply-many methodology. On average, more than 60% of problems are resolved without any customer involvement.

Faster = Better

When the software vendor is also the service provider, Software on Demand problem management processes can be completely reengineered to deliver faster and better problem resolution. Independent of location of the computers, the software company has a direct connection to customers' systems, eliminating the unnecessary step of replicating problems and allowing the vendor to prevent problems from ever occurring. At Oracle, On Demand customers file half as many problem management service requests as their offline counterparts. In addition, once a request is filed, it is resolved on average twice as quickly. But this is all dependent on standardization of the infrastructure, hardware, and software.

When standardization has been achieved, resolution is faster and simpler in the On Demand model because you're not trying to figure out complex problems over the phone and guessing the state of the computer systems. Instead, you know. With this comes a fundamental shift in the problem management process itself. Today, much of the process is buried in incomplete information capture in an asynchronous, haphazard way, and it's driven by whether the detective on the case might have seen the problem before. As with a rookie detective, he might follow a lot of dead ends, waste a lot of time, and never come to a resolution.

A move beyond people-powered to computer-powered problem management lets computers tell us what the state of the system is, rather than us trying to guess. It lets computers drive us through a problem management process rather than trusting the best intentions of a rookie support person. We think it's silly for anyone to call *Car Talk* to diagnose a car problem. When will we think it's equally silly to do that for managing problems in complex computer systems?

Software will always have bugs, but the root of much of production system instability is change. Given the fragile patchwork nature of many corporate application environments, making and managing change surfaces as the single most difficult problem.

8

The Quick Change Artist

In today's business environment change is truly a constant. Organizations must continually keep up with the latest technology and services trends to remain efficient and competitive. However, many times companies struggle to make changes in their software in a timely, cost-efficient manner. Typically, when a company is implementing a complex software system, the first 6–12 months are painful as the company fights to achieve stability. Because that part is so painful, the answer to any change request to add a security patch or new functionality is, "Don't touch it." This goes on for years. Sadly, the software company produces new releases of software with new functionality, but it can't be used because of the "Don't touch it" mantra. One day, the software company declares an end of life. SAP recently stated that R/3 versions 3.1i, 4.0b, 4.5b, and 4.6b won't be supported under regular maintenance plans after December 2003. With this desupport, corporations are faced with huge upgrade costs. And the cycle continues.

Traditional IT outsourcers like EDS and IBM don't help the problem because, from their point of view, change equals cost; therefore, the less change the lower the cost and the greater the reliability. That's good for non-strategic systems that are set in concrete, but how can this be good for the computers a business depends on? On the other hand, software companies want corporations to embrace change, taking the latest functionality and reducing the software companies' cost of support and maintenance. This is why, perhaps more than the other five horsemen, change management in the software on demand model engineers for change, plans for change, and embraces change—which is good for the user and the producer of the software.

This chapter outlines some of the historic challenges to change management and shows you how change management is implemented in Oracle's On Demand model. We'll also discuss one customer's experience and give you a glimpse into the next generation of change management powered by computers, not people.

Let Someone Else Be the Guinea Pig

Change is difficult and costly. Kevin J. Connolly heads up Connolly Architects of Milwaukee. His firm was using AutoCAD Release 14 when Autodesk released the first version of its Architectural Desktop (ADT 1.0). Connolly was wary of ADT because it represented a major change in features and function compared to AutoCAD Release 14. "We intentionally stayed away from it," Connolly recalls. "When ADT 2.0 came out, we upgraded to that version," he says, confident that any bugs in the program would have been fixed by the second release.

Connolly's firm has since switched to a new design platform—Graphisoft's ArchiCAD—but he still refrains from adopting every major software release as soon as it hits the market. Connolly believes new-release bugs are endemic in the industry, not an ailment of any one vendor. "When a big new version of ArchiCAD comes out, maybe we'll take every other one of those," he says.

Connolly's wait-and-see attitude isn't unique to small firms with modest IT resources. Some technology managers at multiple-division companies that employ hundreds of CAD users take a similarly restrained approach to the regular incremental and blockbuster upgrades common among software vendors who serve architects—even adopting, like Connolly, the philosophy of installing every other new release. "I like to be number two and let somebody else do the debugging," says Michael Walters, director of IT in the New York office of Perkins & Will.

It's a Big Deal

In the highly competitive and innovative world of software development, regular changes to applications are a fact of life. No one can blame architects for being cautious. The initial cost of upgrading CAD software, for example, can range from $200 to $600 per workstation. Multiply that by the number of CAD users, and the bill quickly climbs into the thousands of dollars. But that's just the beginning.

Additional costs accrue from hardware upgrades. Often, new software requires users to pack their machines with more memory and storage capacity. In some cases, a newer, faster CPU is necessary to effectively run the revision. "Hardware upgrading is one of the scariest parts [of adding new software]," says Michael Horta, principal of Computers in Design, a New York–based training and consulting company. "Do you buy new machines or spend $2,000 to upgrade existing computers?" He notes that the minimum hardware recommendations provided by vendors aren't always practical. "Whatever the box says, automatically double that," Horta advises.

And Then There's the Training

Even if you can swallow the cost of buying the new software and upgrading your boxes to run it, you must also consider personnel costs. The CAD specialists we've been talking about might need 4–8 hours of instruction (at $30–$40 per hour) to learn the software's new capabilities. Chris Barron, AIA (vice president of architecture for Graphisoft) recommends budgeting for training costs at two times the price of the software upgrade. Putting new features into practice takes even more time. "You take your production person, who is running 80 miles an hour and cut them back to 50 miles an hour [while they learn to use the upgrade]," says Horta. "Do that across the whole office, and it's a sizable cost. A company may not fully benefit from a revision's enhancements until users get comfortable after four or five projects," Horta adds.

So, Where's the Upgrade?

Upgrades have become so complex, expensive, and integral to business processes that the term *upgrade* can be a misnomer. According to Gartner, Inc., enterprise software upgrades can cost up to 30% of the original software installation price, take more than a year to complete, and require companies to revamp their technology infrastructures and business practices. CIOs have to present a strong business case for why, in these difficult economic times, their company should go through the trouble and expense. That's a tough sell to most corporate boards.

Software changes are complicated by evolution—or revolution—in the fundamental underlying technologies. The last big underlying technology move was the move from a client/server architecture, in which PC-based software accesses a central server through a company's network, to an Internet architecture, in which a Web server joins the mix and the software is accessed through the public Internet and a Web browser. It's new turf for both IT staffers and end users.

Staffers suddenly must see the Internet as the platform for the company's most important applications. End users must learn different ways to access programs and absorb all the business process changes that come when they can collaborate with people outside the company. These added capabilities are a good thing, of course. But the required planning and change management make them a migraine minefield. But this is only the latest step. Up next: Intel architectures, grid computing, and Linux. Get the Advil ready.

This Tape Will Self-destruct in 10 Seconds

Even if you decide that you can live with your current systems indefinitely, you might not have that option. The so-called "desupport date" is the ticking time bomb of enterprise software upgrades. Most vendors establish a date after which they will no longer support a given version of their software. Technology changes and customers—especially new ones—demand fresh functionality, and software companies can't afford to simultaneously support six different versions of their software.

CIOs might challenge desupport dates, especially the surprise desupport announcements that most major vendors have made in the past few years. CIOs believe they aren't getting enough time to perform one upgrade before a vendor announces a desupport date for an older version. Nextel's Dick LeFave has been through this. "When the vendor comes to you and says the product is at the end of its life cycle, that's code for saying, 'I'm going to be putting my maintenance and development resources on a new product, and you're not going to get anything unless you pay for it yourself,'" he says.

Even if the vendor continues to support old software versions, it usually shifts the bulk of its people and resources to new versions; therefore, finding someone knowledgeable about the old version is as difficult as trying to find a department store salesperson on red-tag clearance day.

And the Hits Keep Coming

Further exacerbating the issue, the average time between upgrades has shrunk from 3 years in the early 1990s to 18–24 months, according to AMR Research. CIOs have lost the ability to keep up. "Vendors are pushing new code out as fast as they can—so rapidly that you may have updates coming at you almost monthly," says Pat Phelan, an ERP analyst for Gartner, Inc. "The vendors don't seem sensitive enough to the fact that the average buyer can't absorb that kind of change."

Whoa, There

With all these difficulties, a few brave CIOs are fighting to push back the desupport dates. In July 2001, 58 members of the 2,200-member independent Oracle Applications Users Group (OAUG) signed a petition urging Oracle to extend the support date for version 10.7 of its ERP software from June 2002 to December 2004. This petition came after Oracle had already extended the desupport date for 10.7 from June 2001.

In the end, Oracle and the OAUG compromised and the desupport date was extended to June 2003. Similar to Oracle, the other major enterprise vendors—J.D. Edwards, PeopleSoft, SAP, and Siebel—have released ambitious upgrades of their software in the past few years and have all extended desupport dates for previous versions in response to customers' complaints about bugs and performance.

The Lady or the Tiger

In many ways it's a trap both for the software company and the software consumer. CIOs have two choices when it comes to upgrades: go along or fight. Unfortunately, both options require more planning than most CIOs do now. Even if upgrades aren't a continuous process—even though some overworked CIOs might think they are—planning for change must be.

But, as the poet said, don't stop thinking about tomorrow. Some companies put off upgrading their enterprise software because the process is a shock to their system—not just the IT system but the business system. Some postpone the process until they will lose support for an old software version if they don't upgrade. To avoid desperate upgrades, CIOs need to create a continuous planning process that includes users, not just IT.

Having a continuous internal planning system for upgrades lets CIOs more easily limit the number of outside consultants they need to bring in to help with upgrades. An AMR study found that companies that handed over responsibility for their upgrade projects to outside consultants spent twice as much ($2.3 million versus $1.5 million) and took longer (10 months versus 6) than those that kept the project leadership and as much of the work as possible in-house. "The costs skyrocket because you will have people on the project who don't know your business," says Judy Bijesse, an analyst at AMR Research. "And you'll have a lot of consultants who are being trained while you're paying them."

The stakes have risen for enterprise upgrades. These projects need to add value, and value is no longer defined by squeaking through an upgrade before the desupport date for an older version. But old habits die hard. Amazingly, 21% of the AMR survey respondents sold their enterprise software upgrades to their business based on vendors announcing desupport dates for the software. That's not planning. That's desperation. If you have a multimillion-dollar ERP system, you need a better reason for upgrading than the fact that the vendor won't support it anymore.

The Clock Is Ticking

The time spent on upgrading enterprise software varies little between small- and large-scale projects. Expect to spend a year or more from the time you begin pondering an upgrade to getting it running. Just determining whether to upgrade your existing system or to choose another solution can easily take 6–8 months. Matching your business processes to the software and deciding what changes are required can take 6–9 weeks. Getting the new hardware and networks up and running and the software loaded in all your locations is one of the easier parts, but it will still consume 4–8 weeks. Given that enterprise software packages are highly integrated and that new enterprise releases can be buggy, the testing phase is a nightmare. Leave 6–9 weeks for that critical step.

Even if all the technical steps go well, an upgrade can fall apart if users don't like the new screens they see or can't figure out how to do their jobs with the new system. Even small changes to the system can mean big changes to business processes and can drive end users nuts. If all goes well, the cutover can be scheduled for a weekend— preferably a long weekend. Fortunately, the same technological advancements driving all this change can provide a better way to deal with it.

Graceful Change

Software on demand takes a different view of change management. Change is not to be avoided; change is to be embraced. We all know the typical scenario. So, it's no wonder that after implementing any version of software and surviving the fight to achieve stability the phrase most commonly heard is, "It works. Don't touch it."

Unfortunately, this has three negative implications. First, the software company is building new features and functions, but the customer can't take advantage of them. Second, the cost for management increases because, as you move to later releases to fix bugs, workaround after workaround must be found and supported. Finally comes the day of reckoning when the software is no longer supported—remember Peoplesoft 7, Exchange 97, Oracle 10.7—and the CIO is faced with a huge upgrade cost and a fixed schedule set by someone else.

It's easy to understand why traditional outsourcers and internal IT departments have attempted to ensure that change is kept to a minimum. Software companies want to keep customers on the latest versions of their software. Moving customers forward ensures that they will continue to be able to use the latest software and reduces the overall cost of support of the software.

As a result, the software on demand model ensures that software is upgraded on a regular basis. Because these upgrades are planned and follow a set schedule and pattern, they are far less disruptive than the ad-hoc or forced upgrades businesses often face. For example, Oracle's On Demand service has performed more than 300 upgrades of the E-Business Suite. These upgrades have been done repetitively with specialized teams following a predefined outsourcing life cycle. So, what have the customer experiences been?

Hot Off the Presses

It takes several tons of steam heat to produce even the thin sheet of paper you're reading this story on. For all the paper globally pumped out in mills each year, it takes a veritable volcano's worth of hydrothermal energy. That's the kind of steam heat the equipment manufactured by Kvaerner Pulp and Paper produces.

An independent division of the Norwegian-owned, London-based Kvaerner Group, which also has its hands in oil and gas, engineering and construction, and shipbuilding, Kvaerner Power is one of the world's leading suppliers of boilers and evaporation plants to the pulp and paper and power industries. In 2001, the manufacturer pumped out revenues of NOK4.8 billion (US$700 million) through its operations in the Americas, Australia, Asia, the Middle East, Russia, and Western Europe.

Driven by a need for increased functionality and integration from its software applications, Kvaerner Power's management decided to upgrade to Oracle E-Business Suite Release 11*i*. "Now, instead of working from information in standalone silos," says Woody Muth, the company's IT director, "we can see the big picture on a daily basis." Before upgrading to Oracle 11*i*, Kvaerner Power's invoicing was a manual operation that could take as long as five weeks to turn out an invoice. "Now, we recognize the revenue immediately when orders are shipped," says Muth. "And our ability to see the overview has reduced the inventory we need to carry by 30%—almost a million dollars." As we've discussed, in a typical business, such an upgrade would take a year or more and would require adjustments to business processes, technology infrastructure, and user expectations.

Commenting on what the upgrade was like using Oracle's On Demand, Muth replied, "I went home on Friday, power-washed my driveway on Saturday, came in to work on Monday—it was the easiest upgrade I ever did."

Constant Motion

But this is only the beginning. Changing software is part of ongoing business for all software companies. On a periodic basis, software companies build new releases of software, and that software must be ported onto multiple environments and tested. Oracle has been doing this since the founding of the company. Today, Oracle delivers 160+ releases a year of five base products and patch set releases on 14 platforms. These platforms are Solaris64, HPUX (PA-RISC), AIX 5L, OS390, VMS, Tru64, HPUX (IA64), Linux (AMD64), Linux (IA32), Linux (IA64), Linux (zOS), Apple MacOS, Solaris (IA32), and Linux (p-Series).

We've developed a sophisticated combination of technology, people, and processes to guarantee that our solutions work in every configuration we can think of so that installation and management remain as simple and consistent as possible. By applying the principle of engineering for automation, we can apply more (and more consistent) energy to change management than would be possible with almost any number of people. Here's a quick glimpse into how Oracle has organized change management into a "factory" approach.

The automated change management factory people are located in Redwood Shores, California; Dublin, Ireland; and Bangalore, India (remember our doctrine of the best people in the time zone?). The current capacity of the factory, which has evolved over the last 3 years, is based on a successful global engineering model in which the various teams are able to work in a 24/6 mode. This ensures quick turnaround on activities that are important to complete in a 24-hour cycle, more or less like daily builds.

As an illustration of the capacity and throughput of the change management factory, consider the eight Unix platforms for a single database release. On a daily basis, Oracle database server developers either add new features or enhance existing features and check that into a common source control system. The source control system is similar to an anchor point for all platform activities. At 2 a.m. PST every day, a label is announced. The automated build processes starts and the team in Ireland monitors it. If there are build issues, they are either resolved by the team in Dublin or flagged for developers in the United States to fix starting at 9 a.m. PST every day. If the build broke because of some issue in the new code that the database server developer checked in, that can be highlighted to R&D, as well.

The QA process followed is a round-robin mechanism in which, over a given week consisting of six work days in the 24/6 model across three countries, the QA runs are scheduled to cover all QA tests across all platforms on a given day. The next day of the week, the round-robin algorithm schedules tests on platform 1, on platform 2, and so on. This provides complete coverage on all platforms within one week. This round-robin mechanism uses about 200 CPUs to successfully execute all the tests every week.

In aggregate, the change management factory builds 666 million lines of code and executes 1–2 million tests of that software per week. Given this automated change management factory, Oracle can ensure that changes to software are made using engineered practices, enabling the software users to have access to the latest functionality and avoiding any large upgrade costs. Transforming software change management from a people-powered process dependent on hiring and retaining the best people (and hoping they don't make mistakes) to a computer-powered process has become the focus of many of the top technology companies and universities worldwide. Automating change, problem, security, availability, and performance management will enable the industry to free investment dollars that have been focused on keeping the plumbing working to higher-value pursuits.

The story does not end outside the software company. With the advent of advanced ubiquitous networks, the stage is set to end not only the traditional people-powered model for managing software, but also traditional software development practices.

9

Repeal Brooks's Law

Throughout the past five chapters, we have been focused on discussing the challenges of managing the availability, security, performance, problems, and change of software in the field. With increased degrees of standardization, repetition, and automation, we can end people-powered software management. This is true whether a CIO chooses to manage the software herself or a traditional outsourcer moves to using higher degrees of standardization and automation.

This chapter goes back further in the story to the source—to the software company, the author of the software. Many of the challenges software companies face in producing reliable, high-quality software to suit a customer's needs are fundamentally reshaped in the software on demand model. To understand that, we'll start with a classic model of software development, show how companies such as Oracle and WebEx are already reshaping the software development paradigm, and finally help you understand the fundamental underlying shift in the economics of the software business afforded by the software on demand model.

Brooks's Law

Few books on software development have been as influential as Fred Brooks's *Mythical Man Month*, originally published in June 1975 and now available in a 20th Anniversary Edition published in 1995. Much of Brooks's original book was based on his experiences as the development manager of IBM's OS/360. Originally developed in the mid 1960s, OS/360 was at the time the largest single software development project ever undertaken. He recounts that the project could not be considered an unqualified success. He writes of several flaws in the design and execution of the system and ultimately concludes that the project was late, well over budget, and underperformed expectations for the first several releases. Not much has changed in the nearly 30 years since Brooks wrote those words.

Brooks documented what later came to be known as Brooks's Law: "Adding Manpower to a late software project makes it later." Many in the software business can testify to their personal experiences that validate his comment. Brooks furthermore estimated that any software programming project's schedule could be broken down as follows: One-third of the scheduled time is spent on requirements, one-sixth is spent on coding, one-fourth is spent on unit testing, and one-fourth is spent on system testing. Assuming a 2-year release cycle, according to Brooks, you'd spend 6 months in requirements, 3 months writing code, and the last 12 months testing. Most people in the software business know that writing the code is easy. However, knowing what to build (the requirements) and making sure the code works (the testing) is where all the work is.

The Werewolf Lives

In April 1987, Brooks published a landmark paper titled "No Silver Bullet Essence and Accidents of Software Engineering" in *IEEE Computer Magazine*. In the paper he writes, "Not only are there no silver bullets now in view, the very nature of software makes it unlikely that there will be any—no inventions that will do for software productivity, reliability, and simplicity what electronics, transistors, and large-scale integration did for computer hardware. We cannot expect ever to see twofold gains every 2 years."

Throughout the past 30+ years, the industry has struggled to find a way to uncover Brooks's elusive order-of-magnitude improvement in software productivity. Rapid prototyping, object-oriented programming, program verification, and Software Engineering's Capability Maturity Model (CMM) all have been thought to be the silver bullet, but unfortunately, each attempt has come up short—hence, Brooks's conclusion that there is "no silver bullet."

The Silver Bullet

However, the software on demand model seen from the point of view of the builder of the software *is* the silver bullet. Let's start by considering the end of Brooks's model and go backward. In the traditional software development model, software is released to alpha customers. *Alpha customers* are typically users who are willing to take buggy software in exchange for the ability to shape the software. After the software has passed through a small set of alpha customers, it is shipped to a larger group of beta customers. *Beta customers* are also willing to take some level of risk in exchange for early access to the new features and functions.

Only after these two additional steps is software typically ready for first customer ship. As Brooks notes, first releases are full of problems, so most customers wait until the software has aged. The alpha and beta phases of most software releases are refined as the software creator and users try to figure out through phone calls and accumulated knowledge what is going on in a complex software system. Users are typically asked questions such as the following:

"What patch are you on?"

"Can you reproduce that problem?"

"Would you reinstall that DLL and try again?"

"What release of the OS are you on?"

These questions are all asked sequentially until enough information is accumulated to diagnose and repair the problem. In our new model, we can completely eliminate this process because much of the back-and-forth is spent trying to get a picture of the state of the overall system. Software on demand spells an end to this traditional high cost process by replacing a patchwork of guesses with full and complete knowledge. The new development model argues that, with more timely and complete information, the software company can significantly reduce the time and money spent in the alpha and beta stages. Early evidence from experiences at Oracle and WebEx continue to substantiate this conclusion.

The Testing Phase

Take yourself back one more phase in Brooks's life cycle to unit and system testing. One of the biggest software development costs is hiring software test developers, building tests, executing tests, and hoping that the coverage of these tests represents real-world experiences. By Brooks's model, in most software development shops, 50% of the development time and more than half of the cost are devoted to testing. During the system test phase, the Car Talk model is played out again between test engineer and development engineer—ask a few questions, make a guess, tell a few jokes, and hang up. Once again the software on demand model ends this paradigm.

Next-generation Testing

The software on demand model ends the traditional testing that consumes enormous resources. At Oracle, we are extracting key business flows from production environments. These business flows are used during the unit and system testing of our applications. Consider the implications of this step:

- The software company reduces the cost of testing. Rather than hiring a test engineer to write fictional tests, the tests are actual business flows.

- The tests are much more effective because they model real-world usage of the software. Clearly, this benefits not only the On Demand customer, but also the traditional customer.

- As On Demand customers are moved to the next major release, the risk is significantly minimized with software tested at the factory rather than in the field.

We're just scratching the surface on changing the software test life cycle, but this clearly represents a significant shift from the disconnected world of traditional software development.

Deciding What to Build

But change is not limited to testing. Let's move all the way back to the requirements phase, which Brooks pegs at 25% of the development cycle. In the traditional software development model, software companies send product managers out into the field armed with surveys and Excel spreadsheets to try to determine what the customers need. This process is expensive, inefficient, and prone to error.

In the software on demand development process, the relationship with the customer is completely different. The software company no longer has an arms-length relationship separated by a long supply chain of middlemen. This model collapses the supply chain, eliminating the middleman. A simple example of this is Oracle's CEMLI framework. By studying the CEMLIs created by the Oracle On Demand customers, we can conclude which reports, forms, and extensions customers need beyond the current functionality. Common requirements can then translate to new functionality in the next release, with change management provided in the software on demand model. So, rather than guess what customers need, we can study the systems to find out.

It's a Different World

There is more. The fundamental model for engineering software has been built on a linear sequential model with a disconnected view of the customer. Even the fundamental tooling infrastructure, configuration management, defect tracking, call tracking, and testing harnesses were all developed with the idea that you could not have complete knowledge of the software. Most defect tracking systems for software are little more than online sticky-note systems that use unstructured text and email to compose a picture of what is going on in a customer's computer system. In a software on demand system, why are we doing this?

The operating requirements and realities of software on demand required early developers to design and develop much of the software development and production lifecycle tools. Min Zhu, president and founder of WebEx, says, "WebEx had to invent nearly 50% of the underlying development life cycle infrastructure because no suitable off-the-shelf platform existed for services development, deployment, monitoring, and maintenance."

When Zhu and his partner, Subrah Iyar, co-founded WebEx in 1996, the concept of software on demand was new. Looking to the telephone network as an example, they recognized that reliable, high-performance audio-visual communication software capabilities would need to be delivered as services. This also meant that the delivery network would be large, complex, and globally distributed. This network would also be continuously updated for any defects, enhancements, and additional functionality, while most of the network would need to deliver services.

After a traditional software product is developed and tested, it is shipped for the rest of the product life cycle to be managed by customers, vendor support groups, and third-party distributors. The life cycle platform for the collection of defect information from the customers, the distribution of patches and other related information, and the process of applying patches have been developed by multiple vendors over the last 25 years. The traditional procedure is designed to handle customers as single entities, and any action by one customer does not affect other customers.

In a shared software on demand infrastructure, a change procedure can instantly affect thousands of customers and potentially millions of end users. Potential problems and mistakes are substantially exaggerated. Although WebEx has had to develop its own software infrastructure, it is only a matter of time before an existing software tool company such as IBM-Rational, BMC, or Embarcadero Technologies or a new software company develops complete life cycle tools for the software on demand model.

Moore's Law

The history of the technology industry has been driven by one central issue: the cost of computing. More than 20 years ago, a little company called Intel was started. Its first products—the Intel 4004 and later the Intel 8080—were thought of as little computers that were fine for game machines or PCs. In 1965, Gordon Moore made his famous observation that the number of transistors per integrated circuit doubles every 18 months. He forecasted that this trend would continue through 1975. The press called it "Moore's Law," and the name has stuck. And as we all know through Intel's technology, Moore's Law has been maintained for far longer.

All the while, the cost of microprocessors has dropped as well. In the end, even though Intel encountered stiff competition, the combination of lower costs for the CPU hardware and higher performance has left Intel as one of the only general-purpose processors for business computing for small, medium, and large companies.

This relentless pursuit of driving down the cost of hardware has also been applied to all the other hardware components. disks, memory, and so on. But what about software? What is the cost of software? And what is the fundamental economic shift that could drive down the cost of software? Shouldn't Moore's Law apply here, as well?

The Cost of Software

To more clearly understand the implications of the software on demand model, you need to be a student of the economics of the software business. Because it is a physical item, most people can visualize the cost of hardware. The sheet metal, fans, microprocessor chips, and disk drives are easily seen as components of the cost of computer hardware. But what about the software? Many people would say the cost of software is zero because the cost to replicate the software is merely the cost of printing a CD. But, as we've seen throughout this discussion, the cost of software is far from zero. If that were the case, a software company would need only an R&D group and a sales group.

In a mature software company, less than half of the R&D group is allocated to innovation; the rest goes to maintaining multiple versions of the existing software, bug fixing, testing, release management, and planning. Beyond this, most software companies have a customer support group that can be as big as the R&D group. This cost and headcount is dedicated to triaging customer issues; tracking problems; and providing advice, education, and other support services.

Software Economics 101

In this section, we will compose an economic model of a traditional software company starting from the R&D dollars invested in building a piece of software and work our way out to the cost of managing that piece of software. To populate our traditional software cost model with data, we will use four public software companies: Embarcadero Technologies, which builds database life cycle management tools; Webex; Oracle; and Microsoft. Because they are all very different companies, they will provide a good understanding of the economics of the software business.

Assume, as a baseline, that the price of the software sold to the end user is $100. In general, most software companies spend 10%–30% of their revenue on R&D. In their last fiscal year, Embarcadero Technologies spent 32%, Webex spent 16%, Oracle spent 14%, and Microsoft spent 12%. Younger, smaller companies tend to spend a larger percentage, although the total dollar number is lower. If, on average, 15% of a generic software company's budget is spent on R&D, it spends $15 to build each $100 unit of software. But how much of that is actually spent on *writing* the software? If we use Brooks's Law as a rough breakdown, $5 (one-third) is spent on requirements, $2.50 (one-sixth) is spent writing the software, $3.75 (one-fourth) is spent on unit testing, and $3.75 (one-fourth) is spent on system testing. Bear in mind that this probably underestimates the cost of unit and system testing because more resources are typically used in these phases.

Although all software companies would like to have just one release to deliver, many old and new releases are usually being managed at any given time. For modeling purposes, consider that half of the R&D budget is spent on new releases and half on old releases. Given this broad estimate, the total number of dollars spent on writing new software in our traditional software cost model is a measly $1.25 out of each $100. This is hardly what most people believe.

Of course, producing software is not the only thing software companies do. They also support the software. In financial statements, this item is called out as *cost of revenue*. Embedded in this cost is the huge labor component involved in assisting customers in managing the performance, availability, security, performance, problems, and change in the software. The four software companies spend between 9% and 25% of their revenue on support. In our traditional software cost model, we'll use 20% as the cost of support. So, for every $100 of revenue, $20 is spent on support.

Finally, we must figure the cost of sales. In our four reference companies, sales spending comprises 26%–50% of the budget. Younger companies typically spend a larger percentage as they invest in growing their sales channel. Assume 30% of revenue as an average number for our model. So, out of our $100 in revenue, the traditional software company spends $30 to sell its software. Of course, if we have a well-run software company, the remaining 35% is profit for the shareholders of the company.

As discussed in the previous five chapters, the cost of software does not end with the software company shipping the product. We'll use the model that estimates the cost to manage the security, availability, performance, problems, and change in the software as four times the purchase price of the software per year. For our $100 worth of software, a customer spends $400 per year in deployment. Assuming a 5-year lifetime of the software, the cost to manage the software per customer is then $2,000. With even a small base of 1,000 customers, the cost to manage our generic software company's software is $2 million across its customer base. Remember that this all started with investing $1.25 in writing the software.

The Recount

A software company executive should consider the difference between the traditional software company and a software company using the software on demand model. Start with the cost of R&D. As we've already seen, the amount of money spent writing software is a small part of the equation. We'll assume that's constant in the software on demand model. That said, there are two significant changes. First, rather than spending money on supporting many old releases, in the software on demand model, we can support fewer releases because part of the design is to provide the change management services to move customers to the latest versions of the software. This reduces costs for the customer, but in this context, it also reduces cost for the software company's R&D budget.

Second, as we have already seen, the cost of unit and system testing dominates the cost of R&D in the traditional software cost model. Why? Once again, whether externally or internally, the cost is driven by test engineers talking to development engineers on the telephone asking, "Would you please reproduce that problem?" "Didn't you know we don't support that operating system?" and "Where is the trace file?" It is not hard to project that the software on demand model could reduce the cost of R&D by 50% and, in our model, take the cost from $15 to $7.50.

Now let's look at the cost of support. Anyone in the traditional software industry will tell you the cost of supporting customers with many variations in releases, platforms, patch levels, and the competency of the humans operating these systems is huge and that our traditional model of $20 out of the $100 might be wildly underestimating the true cost. It is not difficult to project that a software on demand model with far greater degrees of standardization and absolute knowledge of the software environment would reduce the cost of support by more than 50%. But even a 50% reduction would result in a savings of $10 in our generic traditional software company.

The cost of sales might remain constant, but there is a case to be made that the cost of sales is much reduced. What we term *sales* is often dominated by support issues, demos, and trying to explain to the customer what the software *could* do rather than showing her what the software *can* do. Finally, remember that our generic customer buying the $100 piece of software spends $2,000 over 5 years to manage the software the traditional software company sold. We have ample evidence in the Oracle On Demand model that we can reduce this cost by at least 50% versus the traditional management model.

Add it all up and it provides a compelling economic case that the software on demand model will ultimately end the traditional software model. From the customers' point of view, you've reduced their overall cost to manage software; from the software companies' point of view, you've increased their overall revenue by providing more complete service. Add to that the reduction in the overall cost of R&D, support, and sales that we modeled at a minimum of $20 out of the $100. Consider that, by changing the fundamental cost model of software, a software on demand model can enable a software company to reduce prices and maintain margins versus its traditional software competitors. This has happened in the hardware industry—we're poised to see this repeat in the software business.

Bid Now

To see the implications of changing the fundamental cost structure of software, we can examine the case of eBay. Forgetting its business model for a moment, let's look at eBay as a software company. It has built easy-to-use software that allows the user to present items to auction. Its model allows eBay to provide this service for individuals as well as corporations. Let's assume eBay started in the traditional model. It would have built the software, hired test engineers to test it, released it on CD-ROM, and been faced with the problem of how to get it distributed. Let's assume it decided to put a CD in every newspaper in the country—imagine the cost—and then had individuals load the software on their PCs.

Next, it would have set up a support help line that had to answer questions such as, "Why doesn't my Shockwave plug-in work anymore?" and "Doesn't your software work with Windows 95?" and "Why does my system say it's run out of memory?" As with most traditional software companies, it would have continued to hire people, developed a support hot line, and worked its way through all these issues. Again, consider the cost of doing this.

Furthermore, assume that eBay wanted to add a new feature, such as Buy It Now. It would have again faced the issue of how to get all 1 million users to upgrade. Would the Sunday paper be successful in getting the word out again? Let's continue to be optimistic and believe it would have been. However, eBay would have to gear up the support line because questions about debugging the Windows XP problems and the deinstallation of eBay v1.0 would be flooding in the next Sunday. Clearly, eBay would have to charge hundreds of dollars for each auction to recoup the cost for their software. Without the software on demand model, there would be no eBay. It makes that much difference.

10

New Kids on the Block

The change in the software business is not lost on the industry as a whole. Gartner, Inc., predicts that up to 40% of all applications will be delivered over the Internet within the next 2–3 years. Gartner, IDC, and *Fortune Magazine* have all cited software as service, or software on demand, as one of the key megatrends. In August 2003, *Business Week* interviewed a number of technology industry leaders. All were asked, "What technologies are you excited about now?" Oracle CEO Larry Ellison replied, "Sure, Wi-Fi, even 3G, is fairly cool, albeit expensive. But the thing I'm most interested in is software as a service."

Why Does It Work?

The software as service, or software on demand, model would not be possible without two key enablers: the cost of hardware and the existence of a global networking infrastructure. Since the late 1990s, a series of new companies has been built with the software on demand model. As already noted, you could consider Yahoo! and eBay as software as service because, at the end of the day, the fundamental vehicle for them to deliver content, email, auctions, CDs, clothes, or books is software that has been uniquely crafted and delivered as an online service.

Along with these large consumer-oriented players, a group of young companies focused on delivering software as services has emerged. To illustrate, let's consider a few case studies: WebEx, RightNow, salesforce.com, NetSuite, and Open Harbor. In each of these, we'll discuss the general solution the company provides as well as some case studies of customers who have bought into the software on demand model. Let's start with one of the earliest—WebEx.

WebEx: Web Communication Services

Headquartered in San Jose, California, WebEx Communications, Inc., is a provider of Web communication services that enables on-line meetings between employees, customers, and partners in the software as service paradigm. To start using WebEx services, you need only a browser and an Internet connection. Founded in 1996, WebEx is now a leader in online meetings and Web conferencing services. WebEx serves thousands of customers around the world, including Boeing, BEA, Agilent, Kodak, and Kyocera. In April 2003, *Forbes* announced that WebEx has been the fastest-growing technology company over the last 5 years, based on a compounded annual revenue growth of 186%.

When you speak to WebEx customers, they tend to give you two reasons for selecting the service over traditional software products. First is the fact that WebEx meetings are a critical part of their business communications and, by working with a company that special-izes in Web communications, they get higher levels of reliability, scalability, and performance. Second is the simplicity of working with a service provider and the ease-of-use of the WebEx service.

An excellent example of a company that selected WebEx for its Web communications expertise is Ashland, a Fortune 500 transportation construction, chemical, and petroleum company. Before choosing between a traditional software-only solution and a software on demand service, Ashland conducted an extensive pilot program. During the pilot, it became apparent that maintaining a server would require significant IT resources. It was obvious that an internal solution would require additional infrastructure, unique expertise, and extra staff. Another key concern was quality and reliability. According to Tom Reeder, manager of corporate administrative systems at Ashland, "For our users, reliability and stability are critical. It has to be easy, it has to always work, and it has to be available on a moment's notice. That takes a lot of care and feeding to get from an internal solution. As a service provider, WebEx does a terrific job." A few months after rolling WebEx out to the organization, Ashland conducted a survey to measure the new service's ROI, and the survey showed an average ROI of more that 3,000%. This kind of huge ROI is not typical of traditional software solutions. Ashland recently upgraded its service to WebEx Enterprise Edition and expects the use of WebEx to continue to grow as the company finds new ways to use the service.

Fiserv Lending Solutions, a business unit of Fiserv and provider of loan origination and processing software systems, selected WebEx's service-based model for its simplicity and ease-of-use. According to Dan Welbaum, Fiserv's senior vice president of sales and marketing for easyLENDER products, they are especially pleased with the fact that WebEx is a completely Web-based service. He said that a few years ago, his group tried a software system that offered basic Web meeting capabilities; however, that product required users to install special software and was awkward, unreliable, and slow. "WebEx is immediately available to anyone with Internet access. There's nothing to install. And there's virtually no learning curve or training required to join a meeting. It's extremely intuitive. Our staff and customers love the convenience of a WebEx meeting." WebEx now serves as a leading sales and training resource for Fiserv Lending Solutions. "It started with sales—we realized that we were saving thousands of dollars a month in travel expenses," added Welbaum. Now WebEx is being used in multiple Fiserv business units and is helping the company boost productivity across the organization. The ease-of-use comes from the fact that WebEx development and the users of WebEx are no longer divided by a huge supply chain of product support people, customer support people, application administration people, and so on. Instead, the supply chain goes directly from user to producer—a huge change from the traditional software model.

RightNow: Customer Service and Support

RightNow Technologies is a provider of customer service and support software as a service with worldwide customers. Founded in 1997, RightNow is a privately held company based in Bozeman, Montana. Its customer service software is built to be delivered as a service. As a byproduct of the company's software on demand model, the average deployment time from customer commitment to being live for call centers of up to 500 seats is less than 40 days, including integration and customization.

RightNow provides a suite of multichannel customer service and support solutions that captures, tracks, assigns, and manages customer service interactions from initial contact through resolution. Using RightNow's case management, Web self-service, email management, and live chat/collaboration modules, companies can achieve a 10%–30% reduction in calls and a 50%–70% reduction in emails.

By using RightNow, Delta Employees Credit Union has seen an email reduction of more than 80% and its monthly phone volume drop by approximately 5,000 calls, while its customer base has grown. First Tech Credit Union estimates that RightNow is saving its company 250 hours a month in employee productivity. MyFamily.com was able to reduce the number of staff responding to emails from 15 full-time equivalents to 5—even as subscribers grew by 60%—while achieving a response time of fewer than 12 hours for most emails.

RightNow's patented self-learning knowledge base technology plays a key role in optimizing service processes. It facilitates the creation of highly relevant knowledge by allowing actual customer interaction to drive content. When service representatives encounter an issue not already included in the knowledge base, RightNow initiates the creation of a new "answer" based on that issue. This eliminates the need for separate authoring processes and—just as important—ensures that the knowledge base addresses all known customer issues.

RightNow's software as service strategy enables prospective customers to more easily make a buy decision because RightNow can offer them a pilot deployment without requiring a major commitment of resources. Similar to Oracle, RightNow also offers the ability to deliver the software at RightNow or on a custom system.

"Software on demand is more than just another way to implement software. It fundamentally changes both the relationship between the software vendor and the customer, and the economics of purchasing and owning software," says RightNow CEO Greg Gianforte. "Customers want solutions that are up and running in days or weeks, not months or years, and are looking for ways to reduce overall ownership costs. With software on demand, organizations are able to get these advantages over on-premise applications. software on demand is altering the way enterprise applications are being consumed, and today we are just in the early stages of this next evolutionary stage for software."

salesforce.com: CRM for the Masses

salesforce.com was founded in 1999 by Marc Benioff, a 25-year software industry veteran and Oracle executive who left Oracle in 1999 to pursue a simple idea: delivering enterprise applications via the Web. With that vision, and with a team of three software developers, Benioff began salesforce.com—what Steve Jobs would later refer to as customer relationship management (CRM) "for the masses."

salesforce.com was started in a rented San Francisco apartment next door to Benioff's. It received no venture capital investment but was funded by Benioff and his former boss, Oracle CEO Larry Ellison. Benioff gave his company a mission—the end of software. Everywhere he went, he wore a pin that had the word *software* crossed out. At every opportunity, he performed crazy marketing stunts to attract attention, including a now-famous keynote speech in which he constantly changed from a smart suit to a Hawaiian shirt and debated himself on the merits of the old and new ways to deliver software.

What began with a simple vision has grown into a salesforce.com family of Web-based products designed to meet the needs of companies of all sizes. The solutions combine integrated sales force automation, campaign management, customer service and support, and document and file management into a single, on-demand, customizable solution that can be integrated with other critical business systems.

In less than 5 years, salesforce.com has become a leader in delivering on-demand software as service. "Our growth validates the belief in 'the end of software' as well as raises new questions for existing software companies," says Benioff. Driven by the benefits of salesforce.com's software on demand model—a unified, scalable solution without the high costs, risks, or complexity of traditional solutions—salesforce.com now has more than 8,000 customers and 120,000 subscribers in 110 countries running its services in 11 languages. With corporate users ranging from AOL to Zagat, the reasons companies use salesforce.com are as diverse as the companies themselves.

Consider the experiences of Wachovia Corporation. The Capital Management Group (CMG) of Wachovia Corporation is one of the fastest-growing divisions of the Charlotte-based financial services giant. For years, CMG's corporate and institutional services unit used a home-grown database to track and manage information, but the system was beginning to break down—and some worried it was beginning to threaten the group's spectacular growth rate. By the end of 2000, technical difficulties with the sales tracking system were so pervasive that even basic uploading and downloading of data was problematic.

In addition, a significant percentage of Wachovia's growth was fueled by the acquisition of other financial services firms, and the database was simply not robust enough to serve users scattered across a broad geographic territory. The integrity of the system eventually became so compromised that employees simply stopped using it for anything but recording the basic facts on deals they had successfully closed.

Essentially, the sales team had no automated tools designed to help them to sell. "They were on their own, and so they were using everything from notepaper to Post-it notes to individual PDAs to track contacts and sales leads," says John Shope, senior vice president and national sales director for corporate and institutional services at Wachovia. "There was no contact management system, no daily activity planner, no mail-merge capabilities, no way to prioritize prospects, and certainly no way to share critical sales data with other sales reps or management," he says. Without a steady and reliable stream of customer data coming in from the field, management was unable to accurately forecast sales or follow market trends that affected the bank's strategy plans—both immediate and long-term.

The system needed to be replaced immediately. Although Wachovia first considered traditional client/server CRM software packages, Shope found the price tags daunting, and he knew that the steep figures represented just a fraction of what any client/server system would cost to install and maintain. "And, of course, it would be a very long time before we could hit the start button," he says. An article in *Fortune* mentioned salesforce.com's online CRM solution, and Shope was impressed by the joint promises of quick implementation and low cost. Wachovia was spending $70,000–$80,000 a year on consultant fees just to keep the old system up and running. Shope observed that, by redirecting those funds into the salesforce.com solution, the new system would virtually pay for itself.

Wachovia rolled out salesforce.com to two institutional sales teams in May 2001. The entire implementation process took six weeks and included customizing the service, mapping it to the unique demands and processes of the corporate and institutional sales group, and putting employees through training. "It was like a giant broom sweeping away bureaucracy and paperwork in order to allow opportunities to emerge," says Shope.

Today, everything is working much more smoothly. Wachovia's sales reps are already saving 30+ hours a month thanks to reduced data entry and administrative duties. This increased productivity is translating directly into more time spent with customers. "sales-force.com helps us know where to focus our efforts," explains Shope. "We can now identify our most valuable customers, and we can focus on prospects most likely to yield large returns."

NetSuite: Integrated Business Management Software

NetSuite, Inc., is a leading provider of an integrated online software system that allows SMBs to manage their entire businesses in a single application. Evan Goldberg, Dave Lipscomb, Bill Ford, and Chris Blum founded the company under the name NetLedger in October 1998, with financing from Oracle CEO Larry Ellison. Evan Goldberg is chairman of the NetSuite board, and Zach Nelson is the company's CEO.

The company launched its first online financial application software targeting small businesses in 1999. With this solid foundation, the company then broadened the application not only to manage back-office and e-commerce applications, but also to manage front-office sales, support, and marketing activities.

NetLedger continued to broaden its product offerings for mid-size enterprises with NetLedger Advanced Accounting, an online accounting solution introduced in August 2002, and NetCRM, an online CRM solution launched in September 2002. In October 2002, the company introduced NetSuite, the first online business software solution to automate front- and back-office operations for companies with fewer than 500 employees. NetERP—a complete back-office enterprise resource planning (ERP) application integrating order, inventory, and procurement business process automation with financials to provide supply chain management and e-commerce for mid-size businesses—was launched in July 2003.

Since the introduction of the NetSuite product, the company has grown fivefold in revenues and has surpassed the 7,000-customer milestone. The company changed its name in September 2003 from NetLedger to NetSuite to reflect the success of its flagship product. In December 2003, NetSuite enhanced its product by introducing customization features that make its online applications nearly as customizable as traditional software.

NetSuite's products have won many prestigious industry awards, such as the *PC Magazine* Editors' Choice Awards in 2001 and 2002, *PC World* Best Bets 2001, *PC World* 2001 World Class Award, Forbes.com's Best of the Web 2001 and 2002, and *Upside* Hot 100 2002. NetSuite also provides enhanced, integrated solutions through a number of strategic partnerships.

NetSuite provides several products delivered as a software on demand service. Designed around easy-to-use portal views, NetSuite delivers the advanced accounting, warehousing, CRM, and customization functionality of standalone mid-market software applications at a fraction of the cost. It enables companies to manage all key business operations in a single, integrated system that includes CRM; order fulfillment; inventory, finance, and product assembly; e-commerce and Web site management; and employee productivity.

NetSuite has enjoyed numerous high-profile successes. Dupont Air Products NanoMaterials CEO Robert Grashoff and CFO Todd Johnson expect to save roughly $100,000 annually with Web-based NetSuite, largely by avoiding drag on IT staff and maintenance costs of a client/server solution. Startup costs alone have saved the company $500,000. By consolidating ERP and data with NetSuite, Dupont Air Products NanoMaterials has eliminated redundancies and streamlined workflow. NetSuite has also helped executives keep closer tabs on business by providing them with real-time customer data, which allows the company to provide better customer support.

Dupont Air Products NanoMaterials manufactures and distributes colloidal-based slurries for use in semiconductor, hard disk, and wafer polishing applications. Founded in December 2000 as a joint venture of Dupont and Air Products and Chemicals, Inc., the company leveraged many of its parents' resources, including home-grown ERP applications, to get up and running quickly. Unfortunately, these legacy applications created silos of information.

It turned to NetSuite largely because the technology's Web-based architecture fit well with the needs of a global, near-virtual workforce. The company's workforce and other stakeholders can plug in and gain data on a real-time basis. With NetSuite, Grashoff, Johnson, and other executives can monitor the business using executive dashboards that have drill-down capabilities. They no longer have to spend time manually cutting and pasting from separate files to come up with the same information.

NetSuite's bigger advantages were in cost savings and, critically, time to implementation. Johnson evaluated a client/server solution but came away with a host of concerns, such as hardware requirements, software requirements, upgrades, data security, data retention, ongoing maintenance, disaster recovery, and common platforms for accessing file servers. He estimates that this solution would have cost 50%–100% more.

In addition, the client/server solution would have taken 3–4 months or more to implement—an untenable situation for a fast-growth company. With NetSuite, Dupont Air Products NanoMaterials was up in a matter of weeks, with the help of its solutions partner, the KIBAN Corporation. Grashoff says, "The cost-effectiveness and timeliness of the solution came together almost flawlessly."

Open Harbor: Integrated Global Trade Management

Open Harbor was founded in 1999 and provides a suite of integrated global trade management services. Open Harbor's integrated service addresses global trade's unique information and transaction management requirements. The solution is unique in that the software is delivered as a service and the trade content is as well. "We believe that global solutions like these can only be delivered via Web services. With the service model, customers can ensure that they are complying with the most current compliance and security regulations," says Chris Erickson, CEO and president of Open Harbor.

Open Harbor's solution is built on a comprehensive database of real-time international trade content. This content includes more than 8 million compliance rules for over 50 countries representing 95% of global trade. In addition to these rules, Open Harbor maintains the Harmonized Commodity Description and Coding System (HS) and Export Control Classification Numbers (ECCN) for these countries. Open Harbor provides an interactive service enabling a user to enter a description of her product and then be guided through a drill-down process to derive the correct classification for shipping.

The online system saves time, allowing trade experts to focus on real issues and saving money by ensuring the correct classification is always assigned. Trade partners such as contract manufacturers, third-party logistics providers, freight-forwarders, and customs-brokers all share the same collaborative view of trade and transaction content around the world. This simplifies transaction planning and execution within the enterprise and across multiple companies.

Customers have benefited from the solution. One of the world's largest express carriers is experiencing a 50% decrease in process times and expects to save 50% on customs clearance costs. Another customer, a world leader in security systems with customers and manufacturing locations worldwide, anticipates that the Open Harbor solution will generate up to 50% savings in global trade costs. Previously, they reviewed every export shipment for compliance; now they review only the exceptions.

After much study, The World Trade Organization's 4th Ministerial Conference in Doha in 2001 concluded that typical customs transactions involve dozens of parties and documents and hundreds of data elements. With the lowering of tariffs across the globe, the cost of complying with customs formalities has been reported to often exceed the cost of the duties to be paid. In the modern business environment of just-in-time production and delivery, traders need fast and predictable release of goods. To enable this, you must have a software as service model. With Open Harbor, trade-compliance processes such as document creation and delivery are automated, ensuring accurate declarations and timely communication while freeing up resources to perform other tasks.

Conclusion

Many other small companies use the software on demand model. Increasingly, traditional software companies are transforming their businesses. Siebel's recent acquisition of Upshot is an excellent example. It's clear that venture capital investments continue to be made in the software on demand model, whether for infrastructure software or in new software companies architected for the on-demand world. Vinod Khosla, partner at Kleiner Perkins and one of the most respected Venture capitalists, was one of the earliest investors in the area and continues to see it as key in attacking the huge expense in modern IT. Each new software on demand offering, whether from a traditional software company or a new startup, takes one more step toward the end of traditional software management and development.

11

The Debate Is the Rate

The time is right for a major shift in the software and services industries. During the Internet era, a catch phrase was "the Internet changes everything." Indeed, although the bubble might have burst, networking and the continued drive to lower hardware costs are forever changing the software and services industries. The intersection of three forces are at work: changes to the traditional software business, changes to the traditional service industry, and the advent of new software companies that deliver only software on demand. At this intersection, the next step in the software industry will be played out. So far, we have focused on the technological changes, but in this chapter we'll focus on the business changes. This chapter discusses a set of issues and challenges that are equally important to investors in software companies, CIOs, and senior management in software companies.

Traditional Software Business Model

The traditional software business model centers on software license fees. In general, this means customers must purchase a license to use the software either in perpetuity or for a fixed period of time. But remember that, although writing software is a highly skilled task, it is only a small part of the overall task of delivering software. Developing production-level software requires unit testing, integration testing, alpha customers, beta customers, and so on. As a result, software companies license their software but also charge for technical support, updates, and upgrade rights.

A software maintenance agreement outlines what types of software problems are given what priority of resolution, how long resolutions of problems can take, remedies if a problem cannot be fixed, user responsibilities in the process, who can contact the licensor's technical support team, and other items. In time, it became clear that software companies were continuing to innovate and add new functionality to their software; therefore, companies began charging for software update and upgrade rights. *Maintenance* or *product support* refers to a combination of technical support services and rights to acquire future versions (minor updates and major upgrades) of the software. Although prices vary, maintenance fees for mainframe software have traditionally cost 15%–20% of the software list price, whereas Unix-based software fees have ranged from 17% to 26%, depending on the level of maintenance.

Vendors depend more than ever on stable maintenance fees to uphold revenue. Vendors' software maintenance terms often require that the fees be paid according to the total number of licenses. Vendors offer two justifications for this: First, software maintenance fees include the rights to new versions of the software, whose value is directly proportional to the license price models. Second, support is typically provided by a first-line help desk that disseminates its learning to users and whose workload is somewhat proportional to the number of users or other license sizing metric. Most customers are unwilling to drop technical support, even if they are contractually allowed to do so, because they will have to repurchase the licenses later.

Software makers often discontinue support for products several years after introducing them for a variety of reasons. Often, software companies hope to grow revenue through a mass upgrade to a popular product, or they want to cut their internal costs by discontinuing labor-intensive support for an older version. SAP has said R/3 versions 3.1i, 4.0b, 4.5b, and 4.6b (introduced between 1998 and 2000) won't be supported under regular maintenance plans after December 2003.

Customers can still call SAP for technical support, but the software maker will no longer automatically provide them with software updates for tax code changes annually as it does under standard maintenance plans. Like most software companies, SAP also might be slower to help companies solve previously undiscovered bugs in older versions.

The revenue in newer software companies is almost solely comprised of software license fees. However, as these companies mature, they start building a dependable base of maintenance revenue. Over time, the revenues from services—both maintenance and consulting—increase in proportion relative to revenues from licenses. Typically, at some point between the 5- and 10-year mark, healthy and fast-growing software companies are selling $1 in services for every $2 in licenses. Move out to the 20-year mark, and the typical business software company sells $2 of services for every $1 of licenses.

This shift is a good news/bad news scenario. Every young software company longs for the day when revenue is more stable and dependable. However, the sale of a relatively small number of high-priced license contracts is risky. Just missing one or two major sales can create a significant shortfall in revenue and profits. The thought of a high percentage of revenue someday coming from a stable base of maintenance and consulting services holds considerable allure; of course, this is balanced by also having high growth on the license side of the business.

Traditional software company valuations have focused on this license growth. Historically, in addition to PE and PEG, investors have viewed price to revenue and book value as alternative measures of value. Given the low rate of return on the sizeable cash balances among software companies and the relative profitability and stability of maintenance revenues, the maintenance stream can gain popularity as an alternative measure of value. Maintenance revenue streams tend to be highly stable, recurring revenue streams long after new license revenue growth has deteriorated. Perhaps even more than hardware, users have a growing dependence on the software vendor for ongoing upgrades, enhancements, and support.

Given the downward pressure on the price of licenses, this stable revenue stream is of significant value because it can be designed to be a high-margin business. Most of the software business model has been based on the hardware model. In the hardware model, you sell the customer Model A. Model A is installed and the belief is that the customer will end up buying another Model A or that, when Model B is released, she will upgrade. Buying enterprise software does not happen this way—customers are not really buying a discrete product. Instead, they are buying into an R&D stream of fixes, updates, and upgrades. Software with no support, no maintenance, and no upgrades has marginal value. It won't be long before the investment community comes up with ways to valuate software companies on this more holistic view of their business. In the meantime, change is also afoot in the way software companies are licensing the software product.

Evolution, Not Revolution

Traditional software companies are evolving their software licensing models and beginning to add separately priced management services to manage their software. Leading this change in license models is Microsoft. Recently, it introduced Licensing 6, which essentially encourages businesses (or anyone else who buys more than five copies of a single Microsoft product) into buying "software assurance" contracts. The new agreement takes away version upgrades and requires enterprises to pay up-front for a two- or three-year upgrade contract. If customers choose not to do that, they must pay the full price when they do upgrade. Microsoft says Licensing 6 is a win for its customers because they are assured of getting the latest releases at the lowest prices. Customers, on the other hand, say that Licensing 6 forces them to upgrade more often than they'd like to and locks them into Microsoft products at higher prices.

Computer Associates (CA) offers another business case. In the new model, customers have the option of subscribing to Computer Associates software, instead of licensing specific products in predetermined quantities. Computer Associates enables customers to determine the length and dollar value of their software licenses and vary their software mix as their business and technology needs change. Under these terms, customers can use a variety of software products of their choice during contracted periods, including month-to-month arrangements, and with fixed dollar values.

Under this model, CA accounts for contracted revenue over the life of the license term, thereby generating large residual value at the end of each quarter. The new business model will cause CA to change the way it recognizes revenue, but it does not necessarily change the company's overall cash generated from operations.

Although changes to software licensing will continue, all software companies have begun to recognize that, as license prices are increasingly pressured, they must find ways to add more value through service. Many traditional software companies are now moving toward providing more services for their software, but they often do not understand how this will affect their business model. As an established large enterprise software company, Oracle had to engineer a business model that would enable it to transform from the traditional business model. First, the license model was left intact. For the E-Business Suite application software, the customer has the option of owning the license in perpetuity or purchasing a 2- or 4-year term license.

From this point, the customer has two basic choices: manage the software themselves or allow Oracle to manage the software. The price to manage the E-Business Suite is established in a per-user per-month pricing model: Currently, it costs less than $150 per use per month— less than the cell phone bills of most salespeople selling the service. Even though traditional outsourcing models have typically required multiyear contracts, Oracle chose to establish yearly contracts for the services. Multiyear contracts can and have been signed, but the yearly contracting model affords most customers the greatest flexibility.

Given the success of the Oracle model, other traditional software companies, including Siebel and Peoplesoft, have also added service models, arguing, "Who better to manage the software than the author of the software?" Amy Mizoras Konary, program manager for software pricing, licensing, and delivery at IDC commented on the Peoplesoft offering: "Application hosting has evolved from the domain of early adopters into a mainstream strategy for companies looking to focus on innovation and offload day-to-day software application management. Companies need to optimize IT staff around critical business activities. A vendor that can provide reliable services and single-source accountability can help maximize the potential benefits of hosting, including cost savings and risk reduction."

No Baggage

Traditional companies have the advantage of a large installed base, but they also are bound by their current business models. So it is in the software business. We're seeing this in both the movements to Linux and in the new companies architected only for delivery as a service.

The advent of Linux has challenged the fundamental business model for software. If software is free, how can a company make money? Red Hat invests in and delivers Red Hat Linux. The current version is made up of more than 800 individual packages, almost all of which have been developed as open-source projects. All can be downloaded directly from the Red Hat Web site. So, if you can't make money on the software, you have to make money on servicing the software. Red Hat's entire business model is based on the idea that customers don't want to spend money managing a Linux environment, so they'll let Red Hat do that. The levels of support vary, from the limited telephone or Web-based support that comes with the commercial packages, to 24/7 emergency technical support for large corporations. Today, Red Hat's services represent about half of the company's total revenues, which is unusual for a company of its size.

The new companies also have the advantage of starting from scratch. WebEx, RightNow, NetSuite, and salesforce.com all have pricing models that have bundled the right to use the software, the right to have updates and upgrades to that software, maintenance of the software, and management of the software. Consider the implications of the software on demand business model by looking at WebEx, whose margins and growth are dramatic for a software company. As an example, compare WebEx to a traditional software company such as E.piphany.

Both companies went public at roughly the same time: E.piphany in late 1999 and WebEx in mid 2000. Today, WebEx is an over $200 million company at 70+% revenue growth and 30+% profit margin. In the same four years, E.piphany has grown to only half of WebEx's site, with a –30% revenue growth and –25% profit margin (all data from Yahoo!). Of course, these two software companies are selling different kinds of software; however, you can't help but compare the fundamentally different financial profiles.

But I'm an Investor

An investor might ask, "All this service is good, but where are the margins in the business?" The services business has traditionally been a low-margin business with expectations that service companies will have 10% pretax margins as compared to the 30%–40% margins of a software company. This, of course, has driven services businesses to look at lower cost delivery models—hence, the move to offshore outsourcing. But at some point, the key to high margins (or product margins) cannot lie in just reducing the labor component. You can clearly see this in the home construction business. New home construction is dominated by prefabrication and onsite assembly of a fixed number of floor plans in large, multihome developments. Custom home construction has been relegated to a high end business pursued by a few craftsmen.

What does *product margin* really mean? *Product level margin*, or high margin, is accrued by companies that build products—meaning building a product repetitively. If a software product company built a unique piece of software for each company, there would be no product level margins. The same can be true of services. Why should the process of installing an R&D security patch into production (change management) be unique to every customer? Why can't the process be repetitive? And if it can be repetitive, why can't you achieve product level margins? Software product support or maintenance revenue at most software companies is a high-margin business. This is an early indicator that this is possible as software companies take on not only reactive support, but also proactive availability, security, problem, and change management of their software.

Where Is This Going?

The software industry sits at a crossroads. On the one hand it has been enormously successful, spawning a multibillion dollar industry that today generates at least $1 trillion in spending per year in companies around the world managing that software. Increasingly the IT budget is so dominated by the management of the availabiltiy, security, problems, performance, and change of that existing software that there is little money to spend on new software. What has the industry done about this?

Centralization and consolidation of human and computer resources led by the traditional service providers like EDS and IBM Global Services have taken a step in reducing the overall cost of ownership. But as we have seen, depending on people-powered software management while perhaps reducing cost incrementally won't hold up under the demands of a world increasingly dependent on computer systems. Human error continues to be the number-one cause of system failures. We are coming to the end of people-powered software management. If we can standardize, specialize, and repeat the key availability, security, performance, change, and problem management processes, we can turn to computer-powered software management. We're already seeing examples of this level of automation coming out of high-tech R&D labs as well as some of the leading engineering schools.

But this is not only the end of traditional software management once the software has left the building, but is also the end of traditional software development. Little has been done to change the fundamental model Fred Brooks described 40 years ago. As an industry, we still struggle with many of the same challenges. Software on Demand, software delivered as a service, ends the disconnected, long, serial development process and collapses the supply chain between the developer of the software and the ultimate user. Software has too long been built for the needs of one. To quote Mr. Spock, "The needs of the many outweigh the needs of the few—or the one." Collapsing the supply chain will cause software companies to build better software, more reliable software, and lower-cost software. Ultimately this reshapes the fundamental economic model for software companies. We are seeing early examples of this change in existing software companies and new startup ventures. The end of software as we know it is not a matter of whether it will happen, but when. The only debate is the rate.

Index

A

alpha customers, software development, 119

Amazon.com, IT outages and revenue loss, 8

American Institute of Certified Public Accountants (AICPA), audit standards, 83

AMRResearch Group, software upgrade cost statistics, 11

Anderson, David, SETI@home project, grid computing, 47

application synchronization, disaster recovery, 72-73

applications, patch management (SMS technology), 84

ARMOR services (Adaptive Reconfigurable Mobile Objects of Reliability), 68-69

Ashland Oil, use of software-on-demand source (WebEx), 133

attacks

automated tools, 32

consequences, 76

financial losses, CSI/FBI statistics, 75-76

auditing

facilities, 81-82

SAS 70 Type, 83

Australian Financial Review, 20

authentication (passwords), 80-81

authorization (privileges), 81

automated attacks, 32

automated change management factory (Oracle), 114-116

automatic provisioning in grid computing, 57

automatic test pattern generation (ATPG), software testing, 95

automation of processes

software-on-demand model, 24

availability management, 59-60

dial-tone reliability statistics, 64

disaster recovery, application synchronization, 72-73

downtime statistics, 60

fault monitoring (PinPoint technology), 67

fault-tolerant transaction processing

NonStop technology, 65

real application clustering (Oracle), 66

S/390 clustering (IBM), 65

micro-rebooting, 67

Oracle FAST START MTTR TARGET, 68

Oracle On Demand service, 71-72

D

H

T

U - V

W - Z